YOUR OWN SURVIVAL GUIDE

WHY ME?

How to Regain Hope After the Death of a Child

WENDY B KING

Your Road to Recover

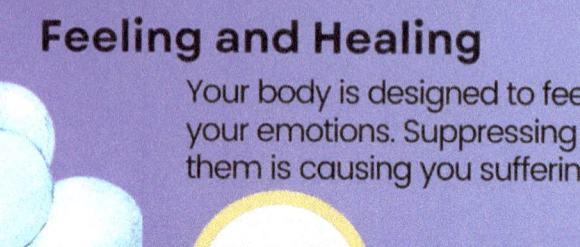

Feeling and Healing

Your body is designed to feel your emotions. Suppressing them is causing you suffering

03

Understanding

What is happening to me?

Why do I feel this way?

01

Growth

Those we love, don't go away,
they walk beside us everyday.
Unseen, unheard,
but always near.
Still loved, still missed
forever dear

04

Accepting

Wishing and hoping that the past could have been different, is keeping you from healing and living life.

02

First published by Ultimate World Publishing 2023
Copyright © 2023 Wendy B King

ISBN

Paperback: 978-1-923123-35-9
Hardback: 978-1-922982-34-6
Ebook: 978-1-922982-35-3

Wendy B King has asserted her rights under the Copyright, Designs and Patents Act 1988 to be identified as the author of this work. The information in this book is based on the author's experiences and opinions. The publisher specifically disclaims responsibility for any adverse consequences which may result from use of the information contained herein. Permission to use information has been sought by the author. Any breaches will be rectified in further editions of the book.

All rights reserved. No part of this publication may be reproduced, stored in or introduced into a retrieval system, or transmitted in any form, or by any means (electronic, mechanical, photocopying, recording or otherwise) without the prior written permission of the author. Any person who does any unauthorised act in relation to this publication may be liable to criminal prosecution and civil claims for damages. Enquiries should be made through the publisher.

Cover design: Ultimate World Publishing
Layout and typesetting: Ultimate World Publishing
Editor: Marinda Wilkinson
Cover Image Copyrights: Art_Photo-Shutterstock.com

Ultimate World Publishing
Diamond Creek,
Victoria Australia 3089
www.writeabook.com.au

Testimonials

Dear Wendy

'I have had what I thought were my darkest moments before, but that moment I made contact with you, I felt as if I was drowning from deep inside me. Today, I can honestly say that I love myself, and I love being alive. Waking up every day is enough reason to be happy and I understand that no matter what life throws my way, I have enough talent, skill, strength and stamina to get through. Life isn't always roses, however, there are rose moments in every day. I wouldn't have gained these strengths without your help, guidance and insight. I see the light in my eyes that you spoke about those months ago, I see it and it is getting brighter. I can't thank you enough.' **T. Williams**

'Thank you so much Wendy! You are such a beautiful, amazing coach and I feel so grateful for what you have helped me achieve!' **Belinda B**

'I will never be able to thank you enough, for the help, guidance and support you have given and shown me. It was so easy to open up with you and tell you some of the demons I have been holding on to in the past. I honestly thought I would take them to the grave with me. You gave me such a new perspective that I never dreamed was possible. You are an amazing lady.' **B, aged 66 years**

'Before I started my course with Wendy, I was struggling to ask for what I needed. I felt I was always looking out for the needs of others, and that I often came last. My life was far less rewarding than I wanted it to be. I was stuck in a rut, not sure how to change things. Once I started coaching with Wendy, I noticed I could use my voice. As Wendy listened and gently asked me the right questions, I was able to identify the areas I needed to change. Some of these were causing me great discomfort, yet I had no idea that I could do anything about it. I found that I could ask for what I wanted and started to believe in my own potential. I highly recommend working with Wendy, if you are someone who wants to gain tools that can be used personally and professionally to improve all aspects of your life, gaining both purpose and clarity in the process.' **Maria B**

Dedication

For my daughter Emma.
Without you, I would not be the person I am today.
You taught me how to be strong, to fight and never give up,
the blessing of what love is, and how to love.

To the mummies and daddies, who have lost a child during pregnancy, during birth, after birth, through an accident, by suicide, or by an act of senseless terrorism; this is for you.

And

My study friend Maree Berzins, who lit the fire within me with her affirmative words:
'Wendy, you MUST write this book, now is the time for everyone to know this. They will learn so much about themselves and discover a way to heal.'

Contents

Testimonials	v
Dedication	vii
A Wonderful Surprise at the end of this Journey	3
Parable	5
Introduction	7

Part 1: My Story — 11

Chapter 1: The Last Days of Innocence	13
Chapter 2: Early Family Life	19
Chapter 3: A Roller-Coaster Ride	25
Chapter 4: Meeting Emma	37
Chapter 5: Welcome to the NICU	45
Chapter 6: Precious Little Time	55
Chapter 7: A Foreign Path	63
Chapter 8: Broken-hearted	67
Chapter 9: My Aching Arms	73
Chapter 10: Grief and Surviving the First Year	81
Chapter 11: Needs as a Couple	91
Chapter 12: An Unexpected Gift	101
Chapter 13: Our Family Grows	107
Chapter 14: Letting Go of the Fear	119
Chapter 15: Thrown a Curve Ball	125
Chapter 16: I'm here with you and for you!	143

Part 2: 12 Lessons for Healing that you Didn't Know you Needed to Hear — **147**

- Lesson 1: Our EGO — 149
- Lesson 2: Our Precious Friends — 153
- Lesson 3: Understanding Trauma — 161
- Lesson 4: How our Brain is Organised and Developed — 165
- Lesson 5: How The Mind Works — 171
- Lesson 6: Understanding our Nervous System — 179
- Lesson 7: Family Systems — 193
- Lesson 8: Children: Emotions and Self-Awareness — 203
- Lesson 9: Who Am I? A Precious Child – We All Have a Wounded Child Within Us — 215
- Lesson 10: I Have Got your Back – Men Only — 223
- Lesson 11: Anger, Forgiveness and Resentment — 233
- Lesson 12: Self-Worth is Your Job — 243

Conclusion — 251
Appendix 1: Scriptures of Comfort — 257
Seeking Help — 273
Choosing a Coach or Therapist — 273
About the Author — 281
Acknowledgements — 285
Recommend Reading — 287
Bonuses — 289

> The hardest part wasn't losing you, the hardest part was living without you.'

Anonymous

A Wonderful Surprise at the end of this Journey

*'Courage isn't having the strength to go on –
it is going on
when you don't have the strength.'*
Napoleon Bonaparte

The death of a child is the MOST painful life experience you will ever feel.

It is unnatural. A child is never supposed to die before their parents. Your mind cannot process it, how can this be? It can't be true! This is not real! How am I supposed to get out of bed, let alone function in some way? I did not imagine my life to be this way.

In its essence, trauma is the lasting effects of emotional shock. You have a new fear: a 'fear of living'.

I want you to know that you are not alone. I feel you, I see you, I hear you. I understand it can be an uncomfortable lonely path. Living with this hidden grief can be so debilitating, and your experience of life now has a new meaning. Grief is so personal;

everyone's intensity and feelings are completely unique. We are all different, but now we have one thing in common, one thing that connects us, we have suffered a trauma – our mind has been changed. Why do some of us seem to cope better in challenging moments than others?

We need to know the answers. In the comforting words of Dr Bessel van der Kolk:

> 'Trauma is not just a story or an experience,
> but it is physical changes that happen in the brain.'

My desire and goal is, that this book will help you grow into an empowered version of you. When you understand that there is more than one reason why you are having difficulty coping, it will begin to make sense to you, why you feel all over the place.

You have the power to learn, to understand, to heal and to discover your purpose: that you can live your greatest truth and open your heart to new thoughts and desires.

Our lives are only limited by our thoughts and beliefs.

If we can trust life – it can surprise you. It is through one step and one day at a time.

Come on, take my hand.

Parable

'The Secret'

There was a large, deep hole, about 4 ft wide and 15 ft deep, in the middle of The Octagon, in Dunedin, New Zealand. In the hole was a sad and miserable elderly drunk calling out for help.

A well-dressed lawyer walked past, stopped and looked in the hole. 'Help me!' cried the drunk. 'Well, you are going to need some legal help when you get out of there,' said the lawyer, and threw down his card. 'My chambers are not far from here. Give me a call and we will see what we can do for you.'

Then along came a priest of an unknown faith. He looked in the hole and listened to the man's pleas for help. 'Well, I cannot help you while you are in that hole, but our congregation meets every Sunday at 9:00 am at the church down the road. you will be made very welcome. Come and enjoy a cup of tea and a biscuit with us, and we will say a prayer for you.' Then, he walked away.

Next to approach the hole was a psychiatrist. He listened attentively and suggested that the two meet when the fellow got out of this hole. He believed a thorough examination of the man's mental health would work wonders. He dropped his card down the hole and walked away.

Then came a doctor. Help was finally on hand, so he thought. Or was it? The doctor bent down and listened but offered no immediate help, other than to suggest the man call the medical centre to arrange an appointment. He, too, reached down and left his card.

Then along came a bloke from AA (Alcoholics Anonymous). He sat down and listened intently for about half an hour. He listened to the man's story and recounted his own. Many similarities later, the bloke from AA jumped into the hole with the drunk.

'Good God man what are you doing in here, now we are both stuck in this hole!'

'Ah, yes,' replied the man from AA, 'but I know the way out!'

Wendy B King

Introduction

What could be worse than not having an instruction manual when your new baby arrives? Not having a survival manual for when your child dies.

When your child arrives into this world, it is a wonderous and scary moment all at the same time. This new person is totally dependent on you, and you need to make sure they are safe and cared for. The problem is, your baby can't talk, and you have to figure out what all the different cries are. Is she hungry? Is he tired? Does she have a dirty nappy? Or is he sick?

You read every baby or child rearing book you can get your hands on, just to make sure you are doing things the 'right way'. Your instincts help a little, but you are also dependant on others who have had babies before you to pass on their advice and tips to help you interpret and understand what this new life is trying to tell you. But of course, nothing can prepare you for the many ups and downs of family life that will occur in the years that follow.

However, there is something far more challenging and overwhelming than navigating parenthood through the years

— it is when your time together is cut short. When you must somehow face the future without your precious child. How do you get your head around that?

Nothing prepares you for that. It was never part of the plan and was never on your mind.

When Emma died, our whole world was turned upside down. It was a sad, lonely and helpless place to be. No-one could give us any sort of answers as to how we were going to feel, or how we could go on. When I was growing up, I never knew of any child dying. Occasionally we heard of very sick children that required medical attention and occasional hospital care, but no child that I knew of, had died. Today, we live in a world where parents in some places send their children off to school and don't know if they will come home. Will their school be the next to experience a mass shooting? The number of these school shootings is beyond comprehension. Too many, far too many. Parents of the victims are now having to deal with the emotional trauma of living each day without their child, and yet they are expected to be a contributing, happy member of society. How can they be if they are struggling to function, both mentally and physically?

The answer isn't simple, but if I can use this analogy to help explain how this beast operates. The beast has two parts. The beast is made up of a house and a hurricane. The house represents you and the hurricane represents your trauma and grief.

If the house isn't built according to the correct building standards, with a solid foundation, the right methods, techniques, and products used according to the manufacture's specification, the chances are that the house is not going to fair very well, in the hurricane, storm, heavy shower, etc. You get my drift.

Introduction

It's the same principle with us. If we haven't been taught how to accept change or deal with our emotions or given the life skills to deal with adversity, then when a storm or hurricane hits (such as losing our child), we are not going to cope very well.

I didn't know how. No-one showed me or taught me how, because no-one knew. Yes, I had a faith, but that was not helping me through my mental or physical pain. So I knew that if I wanted change, I was the one that had to do something about it. I was sick and tired of being 'sick and tired'. I was carrying this invisible weight with me all the time. I didn't want to forget about my child, but any thoughts of her just brought pain. I wanted to honour her memory, not forget her. I wanted to laugh again, but I didn't know how. My emotions were paralysing and debilitating for many years. Finally, about three years ago, I saw an opportunity to learn about my emotions and feelings. So I enrolled with the International Coaching Institute to learn what causes us to shut down or supress our emotions, what causes us to feel self-conscious and how we process our thoughts. I discovered much of our belief systems about ourselves, thoughts and emotions tied back to how we were raised. This then lead me down a path of learning about human behaviour, trauma, the body and the brain. What I have discovered is that everything that has happened in our life, all our experiences, good and bad, the love we were given or not given, the type of partner we choose, it affects our whole being, our whole soul.

Today, I know how to turn my challenges into opportunities, and I want to share my wisdom and the wisdom of others with you, so you not only understand life, but can grow through it and 'feel alive' again.

My intention is quite simple as expressed – in the words of the late author and activist Maya Angelou:

Why Me?

'When you learn, teach. When you get, give.'
Love Wendy B xx

Part 1

My Story

CHAPTER 1

The Last Days of Innocence

*'I am not what happened to me,
I am what I choose to become.'*
Carl Jung

I was 13 years of age and it was my last day of primary school. Everyone in my class was about to head off to various high schools after our summer holiday break. I found this hard to imagine. This was going to be the last day, the last time we would all be together in the same room.

Going to high school was a big deal for most of us, as we had spent the last eight years together. Some of us started on the same day, and over the years we had invented new games together, represented our school in sports together, and shared our loves and hates together. We did pretty much everything together.

There was only a handful of children over those years that had moved away to a new town or school, so we knew each other quite intimately. You could possibly say our school community was our extended family. There was a real sense of belonging.

Why Me?

During this period of my life, I loved school and my friends. Life as I knew it was very free and easy and an escape for me from my very strict family life. I didn't have to be perfect, or seek approval. I felt accepted for just being me.

I was a bit of a tomboy and preferred to play with the boys. They would let me play marbles or bullrush anytime, whereas with the girls, they were either hot or cold. I couldn't be bothered with that. One of my best memories was the day I bought 'ape' bars with my paper money and put them on my Raleigh Twenty. That's right, I converted it. Our school was on a hill and I remember racing down the hill like I was on a Harley Davidson – the boys thought I was so cool. I felt free and cool. Wooohoooo!!! Little did I know, that was going to be one of my last memories where I felt freedom and joy.

For most of us, we couldn't really imagine not returning to Green Island School and that we would soon be split up and embark on our next stage of life.

On our last day of school, we always had a shared lunch. We would all bring a plate (Kiwi language for a plate of food) and sit around at lunchtime and gorge ourselves silly with all the food that was spread out. There was always more lollies and cake than food, but that was what it was all about. It was not normal practice for the teacher to give a speech or lecture, only wish us a safe and happy holiday break. However, as this was our 'last' day as a senior at school, our teacher Mr Henry wanted to share some words of wisdom with us.

His words had a very profound effect on me. They went along the lines of:

'Many of you here today have known each other for most of your life. Some of you will stay friends and some of you will meet new *friends. Some of you will become nurses, doctors, secretaries, or maybe the Prime Minister or a world leader. But sadly, some of you will not have the life you intend to have.*

What I know from the many years of teaching, is that some of my students, have made some poor decisions and died before they were 20. Some have been struck down with a terrible illness, some have lost a parent, or some have succumbed to taking their own life. And some have had very successful lives.

What I am trying to tell you is that the next day is not guaranteed.

Make the most of every day, and think about the decisions and choices you make, because those choices and those decisions, could impact you for the rest of your life.

However, with saying that, you don't always have control over some events in your life, which is usually to do with the law of nature. Some of you will experience some extraordinary challenges, such as an illness or a death, but it is how you deal with it that will either make you or break you, so make the most of every day.'

There was complete silence. I remember looking at the faces of everyone sitting around in the circle. We were quite a vibrant bunch, but you could have heard the sound of a pin drop. I think for most of us, it was the first time that our 'ears' were turned on.

What! Some of us here would not make it to retirement or make it to their twentieth birthday? That just seemed unfathomable.

It was such a foreign concept. But at the same time, we understood what he was trying to tell us. We knew only too well that everything as you knew it could change in a flash. A brother of a boy in our class was tragically run over by a lorry when he was riding his motorbike during the lunch break. Everyone heard about it within seconds, and it affected many families that attended our school. On the day of his funeral the whole school lined the streets to support the family.

That was another thing about our school, there was many older brothers and sisters, and younger siblings attending. It was a very tight-knit community. Everybody knew everyone.

It was big news hearing that parents had separated within two of the families at school. I felt an ache for my friends who had to meet the new 'girlfriend' or 'boyfriend'. I couldn't get my head around that. I couldn't imagine my dad bringing home a new girlfriend or my mum a new boyfriend. So that was big news for us back then. That was about as scandalous as it got.

So, after Mr Henry spoke, for about three seconds there was complete silence. He then finished by saying, 'Now on that note, eat up, it has been a great pleasure teaching you, and I wish you all the best.'

At the end of the day, there was lots of hugs and tears, even from the 'cool boys' as it just hit us that this was going to be the last time that we would be all together. I had no idea how relevant the words of my teacher would be, or what my future looked like. I could not have imagined then that I would have to make a decision to leave home when I was only 17; or that at the age of 25 my first-born child would die.

The phone call that changed everything

Over a decade later, on 25 June 1991 at approximately 4:05 am in the morning, I heard the landline ringing from our bedroom. I nudged Neil. Wake up... wake up, you need to get up, the phone is ringing. It will be for you.' Neil was on standby for a friend to collect the local morning papers from the *Otago Daily Times* and deliver the bundles of allocated papers to the paper girls and boys at the various drop off points. I nudged Neil again. Nothing. 'Neil' I said, 'Wake up, wake up, that will be Brian, he needs you to get the papers this morning for him. Get up.'

While he climbed out of bed, I rolled over. My mind was groggy with sleep. It was the middle of winter and you could hear the wind howling in the trees. It sounded awful outside. I was glad to have a couple more hours to stay in my warm bed.

But within seconds, everything changed. Neil staggered into the bedroom crying and muttering. He was like a possessed person saying, 'No, no, no ... it can't be, it can't be.' I was now wide awake. I turned the lamp on. I have never seen him in a state like that before. 'What's wrong! What's wrong? Talk to me, what's wrong?'

'It's Emma, Wendy, it's Emma! She is dead.'

CHAPTER 2

Early Family Life

*'You will face many defeats in your life,
but never let yourself be defeated.'*
Maya Angelou

So how is this supposed to pan out again? Oh, that's right, you get pregnant, give birth to a bouncy, healthy baby and then live happily ever after as a besotted family! How naïve I was.

Starting at the beginning

The excitement of becoming a mother for the first time for me was euphoric. I was going to have a wee human, a wee person growing within me. I was on cloud nine.

As a young inexperienced woman, I had no idea how your perfect idea of pregnancy and birth could turn out so completely different. I just never considered it. Maybe if we knew the road ahead, and the possibilities of what could go wrong, we may not have had the courage to try, and go down that path.

We had purchased our idyllic first home and life was good. We were taking possession of it in approximately four weeks and I couldn't wait. It had been a great achievement for us both. We had been renting for four years, but had managed to keep to a strict budget so we could accumulate enough money to put a deposit on our first home. This required quite a bit of discipline, but we got there finally!

The next morning when I woke up, I felt a bit peculiar, not sick enough to stay home, but not right in myself. So I trotted off to work. As the morning went on, I started to feel hot, a bit irritable and itchy. But still, nothing alerted me to thinking anything was out of sorts. I wasn't until I went to the bathroom before returning to work after lunch, that my skirt band had rubbed my tummy and caused me to want to scratch like crazy.

Something must have bitten me. On untucking my shirt and looking at my tummy, low and behold there was a very red angry rash. What the blazes I thought? I've never seen anything like this before. Now feeling anxious and not sure what to do, I did what everyone did at 'Housing Corporation' at the time – consult with our resident 'mother in charge' Nancy Gosden, to get a diagnosis. Nancy was a beautiful kind caring lady, nearing retirement who seemed to know anything and everything about all sorts.

'You've got the measles young lady, that's what you have. Best you ring your doctor and get yourself looked at.' End of discussion.

I saw my doctor later that day, and after being examined, it was concluded I had a 'virus'. My doctor was very self-assured. I believed

Early Family Life

him – he was the doctor and I was raised not to question any adult especially someone in his position. I did however mention that it was suggested by one of my work colleagues that I might have the measles. 'No,' he said, 'this is purely a virus. The best thing you can do is take yourself home, take some Panadol and hop into bed. You'll be fine. If you are not feeling any better in the morning, give me a ring.'

I did just that – Neil was concerned but also said, 'go to bed!'

The next day

When I woke the next morning, my skin felt raw from head to toe. I felt as if someone had attacked me in the middle of the night with sandpaper and had rubbed it all over my body. I touched my face; it was sore and tender. *What on earth is going on?* I was home alone as Neil had already left for work.

I moved with caution to investigate my body in the bathroom mirror. Horrors, I looked like a raw meatball, red and blotchy. The rash that was only in the abdomen area had overtaken my body with ferocity.

It was too early to ring the doctors' rooms, it would still be over an hour before the surgery would be open, so that I could talk to the doctor or nurse. Waiting for the clock to reach the opening hour of 9:00 am seemed to take an eternity.

When the receptionist answered, I explained my predicament. 'I saw Dr Borrie yesterday, I have a rash you see, and he did say that if I felt worse to ring today. May I talk to him please?' She explained he was just about to see a patient, but promised to get him to ring me before he saw his next patient.

Why Me?

The phone rang shortly after. 'Wendy, it is Peter here,' he said. 'Tell me what's happened?'

I explained the rash now covered the rest of my body. 'I am so sore and uncomfortable. I feel as if my body has been rubbed with sandpaper. I don't know what to do? I can't go to work or come up to see you, I am in a terrible state, if people saw me, they would be running for cover.'

'Oh dear,' he said. 'The virus seems to have taken hold. Look, don't worry. I will write you a medical certificate to take the rest of the week off. In the meantime, I will set up an appointment for you to see me in a week's time. Then I will know if you are fit to return to work. How does that sound?' I thanked him and hung up the phone.

For the rest of the week, I lay in bed with the curtains closed and slept and slept. I was very lethargic, and nothing interested me in any shape or form.

A week later, my rash was all but gone. I was feeling a little apprehensive. I was looking forward to seeing my doctor for more than one reason. I still felt a bit yuck, but not only that, I was late with my period.

I am never late. I was worried. 'Let's do a pregnancy test,' Peter said. The result was negative. He reassured me not to worry, it wasn't uncommon to miss a period when you had been sick. I was relieved. I wasn't sure how I would have felt if the result had come back positive after being so sick.

Early Family Life

Our new home

So, moving day had come and gone and we were excited about starting our life together in our new house. Our home.

I was in the kitchen cooking dinner and I suddenly started to feel quite nauseous. The smell of the food cooking was really getting to me. My period still hadn't arrived. I served up dinner to Neil, but I decided to skip dinner and just have a cup of tea and a piece of toast. 'Aren't you having dinner?' asked Neil. 'No,' I said. 'I'm not feeling that flash.'

'That's no good, you've had a bit of a bad run lately, haven't you?' he said. I agreed, adding, 'I'm a bit over it!' I took a mouthful of my tea, but it didn't taste right. I can't even enjoy this cup of tea, it tastes weird! I quietly wondered what the heck is going on.

The next day at work, Nancy stopped me and asked if I was feeling okay, adding 'You look a bit peaky.' I explained I was not feeling that flash. I decided to confide in Nancy. She was like the grandmother I never had, motherly, with a big bosom and smiling eyes. She gave the best hugs, and could instantly make you feel that whatever problem you had, it was only half the size it was. 'I still haven't had my period, but I did have a pregnancy test 10 days ago and it came back negative. I can't help thinking what else it could be, as I am feeling a bit squiffy.'

I noted a twinkle in her eye, as well as a concerned tone in her voice. 'I think you should probably have another pregnancy test. You can always make an appointment with Family Planning rather than with your doctor. If the result is positive, they will just forward the information on to your doctor. If you're not pregnant, then all good. It is better to know one way or the other instead of worrying.'

She was absolutely right. So, I did. I rang Family Planning, and they were able to see me the next day.

On my way home from work, I was hoping Neil would get home before me, so he could start preparing dinner. I couldn't face cooking anything, just the thought of it made me feel sick. Man, I thought, I hope this passes soon.

I couldn't think of what meat to start preparing so I thought I would make broccoli and cauliflower with cheese sauce as I was a bit partial to that. Oh, but what a mistake that was! As soon as it came to the boil, oh my goodness. The smell. I felt my stomach heaving. Neil had been in the door only five minutes when I called out, 'You're going to have to finish dinner off. I'm going to throw up!'

That was the end of my night.

CHAPTER 3

A Roller-Coaster Ride

'The problem is not the problem. The problem is your attitude about the problem.'
Jack Sparrow

'What do you think is wrong?' Neil asked. I told him that Nancy said that there was still a possibility that I could be pregnant even though the first test came back negative. I mentioned that I had managed to get an appointment with Family Planning, and a second test would confirm one way or the other. 'Do you want me to come with you?' he asked. I was thinking that it was probably going to be negative anyhow so, I said, 'No, don't worry.'

I was wrong. 'Congratulations!' the nurse said, 'You're pregnant! How do you feel about this news?' Stunned was the truthful answer I was thinking. You could have knocked me over with a feather. 'Gobsmacked,' I replied. 'Happy, I think?'

She then asked me if I remembered when my last period was, 'Just so we can figure out how far along you are?' I was pretty certain when the baby was conceived, as sex had not been all that regular due to being ill and moving house. I asked for a calendar so I could work this out. 'I will forward these details off to your doctor. When you are three months, make an appointment to see your doctor, and he will look after you from there,' she said.

I couldn't wait to phone Neil and tell him the news, I was shaking with excitement, but I was also partly concerned. Neil was ecstatic. 'A dad – I am going to be a dad! Well, that explains why you are off your food and feel like throwing up, hopefully it will pass soon. Love you babe, see you when you get home tonight!'

I can't remember who got home first that night, but we were both incredibly happy. Everything was falling into place. We had only recently moved into our first home, and now we are going to be parents!

However, underneath the excitement, I was nervous about the virus I had when my period was due. Later I asked Neil if he thought it could have affected our baby. 'Umm, good question. When we see the doctor at 12 weeks, we will ask him about it. In the meantime, don't worry, you are going to make a great mum.' He squeezed my hand to reassure me. 'Anyway,' he said, 'we have work to do. Our first project – we have a baby's room to get ready!'

12 weeks, September 1990 – 1st doctor's appointment

'Well, that is wonderful news! Congratulations you two!' Dr Borrie exclaimed. He asked how I was feeling and I explained I still felt a bit nauseous. 'It goes all day really. I don't understand why it is called morning sickness.' My doctor smiled. 'Unfortunately, that comes with the territory, and it varies with each person. Some get it very badly and need to be hospitalised due to dehydration setting in, and others don't have any symptoms at all.' He then asked me if I had any concerns.

I reached for Neil's hand. 'Actually, I do,' I said. 'Don't be nervous,' he reassured me, 'What is on your mind?'

I reminded him of my illness a few weeks ago. 'You said I had a virus, and the rash was really bad. I am just worried it might have affected the baby, as I had missed my period and we did a pregnancy test, but it was negative. I just can't get that week out of my mind.'

'No, no, Wendy don't worry, you just had a terrible virus,' he said. 'You'll be okay, and so will the baby. We just need to confirm your dates. Are you sure when this baby was conceived?'

I was sure. I knew exactly what weekend it was, there was no weekday sex for this tired bunny. He then suggested we go for a scan at 16 weeks instead of 19 weeks to see how things were tracking. I agreed that would be really reassuring, and it would put my mind at ease. 'Okay, I will organise that for you. Now off you two go. And Wendy, I will see you the day after your scan. Alright?' he said. 'Brilliant,' I replied.

As we left the doctor's room and hopped into the car, I asked Neil if he was feeling okay with what the doctor said. 'Yes,' he said. 'Look there is nothing we can do. I am sure everything will be fine, so don't worry. Anyway, I am desperate to tell someone our news. I can't keep this to myself any longer! Let's ring Mum tonight, she will be stoked!' We then chatted about a theme for the baby's room, and excitedly planned to go and choose the paint and wallpaper this coming weekend. I also bought my first pregnancy book as well, so I could understand more about what was going on within my body.

It didn't take us long to choose wallpaper for the baby's room. We decided not to go for a baby theme but a toddler theme instead. Paddington Bear wallpaper with red accents and long white drapes. It was going to be incredible. A beautiful space for our beautiful baby and it didn't matter if it was a boy or a girl.

16 weeks, October 1990 – 1st scan

On arriving at the clinic for my scan, my emotions were all over the place; I was excited, nervous, giggly and apprehensive all at the same time. This is real, I am going to be a mumma! I was still trying to get my head around the fact that there was a wee human growing in my tummy, a baby. I was just in awe of what my body was capable of doing.

By this point I was comparing the size of my tummy with the pictures in the pregnancy book. I was still quite small for my dates. My tummy looked as if I had eaten too much, and I couldn't do my button up on my trousers. My pregnancy book told me at this stage, I might start to feel flutters from the baby moving, but I hadn't felt any movement yet.

'Mrs King,' the sonographer said, 'Come through please.' She showed me to a cubicle. 'Just pop your clothes off here, you can leave your undies on. Just come through to the room adjacent to the cubicle once your gown is on.'

The sonographer gently lifted my gown up to expose my tummy. 'Now I am going to squeeze some gel on your tummy; it will feel a bit cold, but it's so I can move this wand around easily in the tummy area.' She picked up the bottle and squeezed it. It made a farting noise. I gave a nervous laugh. 'It does that to me all the time,' she said. 'Now, just relax. I am going to take some pictures and some measurements of baby.'

Before I knew it, I was looking at baby's heart beating away on the monitor! It was amazing! It looked like a butterfly fluttering. This is the moment, that cemented in my mind that this was real. I wasn't imagining this baby growing inside of me. I was going to be a mother.

The sonographer continued to sweep my tummy with the wand whilst clicking away and measuring different parts of the baby. Then she asked me, 'Do you think there's a possibility your dates are wrong?' I asked why. 'Well it seems that baby is smaller than what we expect at 16 weeks, so I'm just double checking.' I said I was definite with the dates. 'Okay, she said. I will send the results to your doctor. When are you going to see him next?' I explained I had an appointment tomorrow. 'That's good,' she said. 'Okay, I am just about finished here, then you can go and get dressed.'

The next day - 2nd doctor's appointment

When I stepped foot into the doctor's room, he greeted me warmly and asked how I was feeling. 'I am feeling fine in myself, I am not feeling nauseous anymore. However, I am concerned about my scan results. The sonographer thought the baby was smaller for my dates?' The doctor confirmed that he had seen the scan results and my baby was small.

'Well how much smaller?' I asked. 'Well, they think you might be out by three weeks,' he said. I gasped. 'No! Absolutely not! Something is out of whack here,' I said. He assured me there was nothing to worry about, and explained he would book me in for another scan at 20 weeks. 'Another scan at 20 weeks will give us a better picture of baby's progress,' he said. 'Okay,' I replied. To be really honest, I was feeling anxious and worried that something wasn't right.

20 weeks, November 1990 – 2nd scan

It felt like an eternity for this day to arrive. I kept saying to myself everything will be okay, that there had just been some sort of technical hitch with the last scan, this one will be fine. Anyway, I had started to feel flutters in my womb. My baby was definitely starting to move around. It was an amazing feeling, knowing a little life was growing, moving and possibly dancing.

I lay there, my tummy felt like it was in knots. The sonographer asked if I was comfortable and I said, 'Yes, just a bit nervous.' 'Nervous?' she asked. 'Yes, I had a different sonographer for my first scan at 16 weeks and there seemed to be a problem with the size of the baby in relation to my dates.' She explained that did happen from time to time, and encouraged me to try and relax.

I wasn't feeling convinced. But when she said my baby's heartbeat was strong, I was slightly relieved. 'When do you see your doctor again?' she asked. 'Tomorrow,' I said. 'Very good. I will send the results through today for him to review.' Nothing had been mentioned about baby's size, and I was too scared to ask.

The next day – 3rd doctor's appointment

It would be fair to say that today couldn't come soon enough. I wanted to get to the bottom of how my pregnancy was really going. My doctor's body language and tone showed a bit of concern during this visit. This was something I was very good at, that is, learning to read body language at a young age – was I in trouble or not?

'Wendy, remember during your last appointment, there was concern over your dates,' he said. 'Yes, that's right.' How could I forget? 'What did the scan confirm, is everything ticking along as it should be?' I asked eagerly. 'Well, it appears now that you might be out by six weeks,' was his reply. What?! No! I could feel my stomach knotting up, my throat tightening and tears starting to prick my eyes.

I can't really describe exactly how or what I was thinking, but I stopped hearing. Everything in my mind was slowing down, and felt like I was in a movie where the voice is slow and muffled. This wasn't happening, it can't be. I started shaking. Lots of thoughts were going through my head. 'It's okay, don't worry Wendy,' the doctor said, and as if he was reading my mind, he asked if I was getting any movement. 'Yes,' I said. 'I am definitely feeling the baby wriggling around.' He assured me that was a great sign. 'Look,' he said. 'I don't want you to worry. I just want you to take note of how much movement you are getting from the baby. If it appears to slow down, or stop, contact me straight away.'

He booked me in for another appointment in four weeks' time, just before the Christmas holidays as the practice would be closed for three weeks. I was raised not to question anyone in authority; however, I couldn't help myself. I found the courage to ask as I was preparing to leave, 'Are you sure there is nothing to worry about?' I felt so awkward for second-guessing the doctor. 'I'm sure. See you in four weeks.'

On returning to work after my appointment, I searched for Bev. I couldn't help feeling nervous and anxious, I needed someone that I could trust and confide in. Bev was like my adopted mother.

She was the right person to go to for reassurance and a cuddle. She would always listen to what you had to say and never tried to 'fix you'. She is the best friend you can ever have, I so needed her right now.

Over the next four weeks, I literally buried myself in pregnancy books to understand everything about my body, the baby and pregnancy. There was nothing I didn't want to know. The books were consistent in saying that the information published was a guide only and everyone was unique, and every pregnancy was different. This gave me some comfort as my tummy certainly was not expanding at the rate shown in my books. I was beginning to enjoy my food again and I wasn't feeling as exhausted. My energy was returning – thank goodness. This gave me a little bit of hope.

24 weeks, December 1990 – 4th doctor's appointment

Blood pressure taken, urine test taken, weight taken, all good. But my tummy was still looking bloated rather than pregnant. 'You look happy, and you are glowing,' my doctor said. 'Are you getting a lot more definitive kicks or movement from baby?' Laughing, I told him I was. 'Sometimes I think there is an aerobic session going on in there!' He then examined my tummy to check the position of baby. I would be lying if I wasn't worried but pushed those thoughts to the back of my mind, but still asked if everything was alright. As a first-time mum, I just needed some reassurance that everything was going to be okay. 'Yes, you do seem small for your dates, but it isn't unusual to carry near the back rather than the front of your tummy for some expectant mothers.'

He asked if I had any plans for Christmas. 'Yes, we are going camping with another couple in Lauder, Central Otago,' I said. 'Oh, that sounds like fun, you will certainly feel the heat!' he replied. 'Well, have a good time when you are away. No heavy lifting mind, and we will see you in the new year. Just make an appointment with the receptionist on your way out,' he said.

28 weeks, January 1991 – 5th doctor's appointment

When I arrived at my next appointment, the GP was concerned that my bump had not grown in the last four weeks. However, as all of my other observations were fine, nothing further was said. An appointment was scheduled in two weeks, 'just to keep an eye on things'.

30 weeks, 5 February 1991 – 6th doctor's appointment

When I woke up that morning, I asked Neil if he would come to my appointment with me. I just felt off. He agreed and asked if I was okay? 'Yeah, I don't know, I just feel a bit anxious. I also think it will be interesting to see what the doctor thinks of my progress that's all. I can't help thinking about a comment one of the girls at work made yesterday about my tummy,' I replied. She had said that Tim's beer belly was bigger than mine and jokingly asked where I was hiding the baby. She was right. I had been thinking it, she said it. She was only stating the obvious, and in my mind the truth of the matter. It was the first real twinge that all was not well. Neil tried to play it down, but agreed she was right. 'Look, just tell the doctor what you're feeling, and we will go from there.' He headed off for work, promising to return to pick me up just after 10.30 am. As he drove away, I couldn't help feeling very uneasy.

Why Me?

11.00 am at the doctor's clinic

Today, the doctor got straight to the point. 'Yes, Wendy and Neil, I'm not sure what is going on here. As a precautionary measure I am going to request an emergency scan. I will book you in to Marinoto Clinic now. Tomorrow is a public holiday and I want to get on to this sooner rather than later. I will need to see you on Thursday to discuss the results, in the meantime, just take it easy and don't worry.'

Don't worry, I said to myself. Yeah right!

7 February 1991 – 3rd scan

The scan revealed there was a discrepancy in the size of baby with regard to my dates. No surprises there! This needed further investigation. A medical certificate was written for my place of employment to have the next day off work. I needed to be admitted to hospital as a day patient in the antenatal department so further tests could be made, and baby's heartbeat could be monitored.

8 February 1991 – Antenatal ward.

9:00 am: Admitted to the Antenatal ward
9:30 am: Advised that I would be in for the day to monitor baby's heartbeat. It was expected that I would leave and return home at approximately 4:30 pm.
11:30 am: Concerns that baby's heartbeat was a bit erratic – although there was lots of moment from baby.
2.00 pm: Sent for a scan to measure the size of baby, heart rate, and flow of blood to the umbilical cord.

4:30 pm: Visited by the obstetrician on duty, who said that there was a change of plan and they wanted to keep me in for a couple of days, so they could give me a series of injections to help with the development of baby's lungs. Then they would reassess the situation. (Those injections were painful. It was like a knitting needle going into your backside).

It was also suggested that I might be staying in hospital until baby's due date. That could be eight weeks!

9 February 1991

9:00 am: I was visited by the obstetrician to see how my night was and asked me how I was feeling. I said I was comfortable but starting to get a bit anxious, with all the questions being asked. I was beginning to feel like there was more to worry about, than what was being let on. He reassured me that he would keep me up to date with any new information, or change of plans.
11:30 am: The nurse who was looking after me asked if I could get hold of Neil and if he could come soon, as the doctor was coming back to see me about 1:00 pm and he wanted to speak to both of us.
1:00 pm: The obstetrician was very kind but concerned. He advised us of the following:

- Emma's heart rate was stable sometimes, then it fluctuated.
- She was undersize for her term in utero.
- The scan showed that the blood supply from my placenta to her was not performing well. There are three blood vessels that are within the umbilical cord. One had shut down and another one was in the process of shutting down. She was 31-and-a-half weeks old, but the size of a 24-week-old baby.

The doctor recommended for the best interests of baby's growth and survival, that she was better out than in (staying in the womb that is). They were making plans on performing a caesarean section tomorrow afternoon under general anaesthetic. This was because they didn't know what baby's overall condition was going to be like. However, they did confirm that once baby was delivered, her new home for the next few weeks would be in the NICU unit (Neonatal Intensive Care Unit), where she would be under 24-hour care.

The obstetrician was so matter of fact. 'I'll go to Sunday church in the morning, pop home for a quick bite of lunch, then I'll come down and then we'll deliver this baby!'

So, there we have it. It would be fair to say that right at this moment, I was thinking *'Yer aff yer heid!'* (Scottish for 'you're crazy'). This was a lot of information to take in. We were going to be parents – tomorrow! This is not right. I still had at least another eight weeks to go. I was completely dumbfounded. One minute I was only coming into the hospital to be monitored for one day, to now being told, guess what, you are having a baby tomorrow. We were both feeling excited and scared at the same time. Neil was panicking, as sudden surprises are not his strong suit.

We then spent the afternoon, telephoning family that we were going to be parents tomorrow. Emma was going to be the first grandchild for both sides of the family.

CHAPTER 4

Meeting Emma

*'There are two great days in a person's life;
the day we are born,
and the day we discover why?'*
William Barclay

I barely slept that night, I tossed and turned, so much was going through my head and body. I remember sitting there with a cup of tea and then having to put it down, because I was shaking so much.

Breathe in, breathe out, pant – yes you know, the exercises you were taught at the antenatal classes. I wasn't sure if it was going to work, but I had to try something to calm the nerves.

It then occurred to me, that today would be the last day I would feel her moving within me. I pulled my top up and looked at my belly, trying to picture what she would look like. Then I found myself talking to her and telling her that I was so excited to meet her and hold her in my arms. I told her that as a first-time mum, it was such an amazing moment, to feel the first kicks of life within me, and that I would miss the feeling of her wriggling around inside my body. I told her that I would not be awake to welcome her into this world, however she was not to feel afraid, because she was going to have the right people looking after her and that her daddy and I couldn't wait to see her or hold her.

We had so much love to give her. We would love her no matter what.

With that, I received a boot from my wee girl. It was such a kick, if I had not been looking at my belly, I would have missed the outline of her foot where it connected to my flesh. I could have sworn I could have reached out and grabbed it. To this day a feeling of warmth rises within my body, when I think of that moment. It was if she knew exactly what was about to happen!

Sunday lunchtime

The clock was ticking. Not long now and our wee girl would be born. Excitement was now passing, and fear was starting to kick in. Fear of the unknown. The nurse gave me a gown to change into. The doctor would soon be coming to see me again and the anaesthetist had just gone through all the formalities.

In less than an hour, I was being wheeled into theatre. Neil was asked if he wanted to come in but chose to wait in one of the side rooms. My anxiety was beginning to rise within me, and when I entered the theatre room, all I can say is that I was glad I was lying down. I don't know why, but I was only expecting maybe three or four people in the theatre room.

Meeting Emma

However, the room was filled with people – the doctor attending, the anaesthetist, nurses and a few students. Boy did I get a surprise! It was crowded. I was not expecting that. There had to be about 15 people in the room. I had been asked by the doctor carrying out the C-section if I would consent to having some students present for training purposes. Sure, I agreed, but thought that meant maybe two or three students.

You could feel the energy in the room. There was tension, excitement and whispering. My anxiety levels were really ramping up, to the point that I was beginning to get a ringing sound in my ears and my body started shaking. I honestly thought I was going to pass out, before my anaesthetic was administed. I was thinking, it is all on. I just wanted this whole event to be over. I soon got my wish. An anaesthetist was called to administer an epidural.

Emma Louise King was born at 2:30 pm on Sunday 10 February weighing 840 grams.

Approximately five hours had passed since my caesarean section. I stirred to the sound of the chatter of voices, bells ringing and noise. My room was right outside the nurses' station for precautionary measures. Oh my, did I feel groggy. I did not have any control over my body. I swallowed – ouch my throat, it felt very swollen and sore as if I had swallowed a packet of razor blades. I was told this was due to one of the students putting the breathing tube down my throat, and not only that, my stomach area felt as if it had been ripped open.

I couldn't move and started to moan. 'Hello dear,' came the voice of a cheery nurse. 'Now let me see, oh yes you are due for some more meds.' She gave me something amazing for the pain and to knock me out. She also carefully placed pillows underneath my body, arms and legs. I felt like I was on a cloud. She was brilliant! I don't remember anything else until the following morning.

Monday morning – Meeting my wee girl

I woke to something tight around my arm, the nurse was taking my blood pressure and attending to my other needs. She asked me about my pain level and said that once I had something to eat and the doctor had seen me on his rounds, they would take me up to the NICU to see my daughter. 'What an exciting day it is,' she said.

At 10:30 am we headed up. I was finally going to meet our Emma. It felt strange that so many others had meet her before me. There she was. Lying in her tiny incubator. She was like a miniature doll with a pink hat on. To me she looked perfect. She did have wires stuck all over her wee body to monitor her heart rate and oxygen saturation readings. But what caused me to feel alarmed and concerned was the pin prick spots all over her.

I just sat there and just stared at her, I couldn't speak. Wow. Emma was awake, lying there, gently moving her legs and arms. I don't remember exactly how long I sat there without saying anything. I just soaked her up, it might have been 5 minutes or 15 minutes. I was just feeling quite overwhelmed and ecstatic, that only a few hours ago she was growing within me.

A beautiful Canadian nurse named Roz was looking after her. 'Hello Mum,' she said, 'Wow, just look at her. Once I've finished doing her observations how about we get her out and have a cuddle – skin to skin.' (This was known as the kangaroo cuddle – I open my shirt and she lies face down with her chest on my chest). 'Really?' I said. Of course I wanted to, but she looked so

Meeting Emma

fragile. Sensing my hesitation, Roz reassured me. 'Even babies this size are stronger than you think. It is important for both Mum and baby to bond.'

As Roz unclipped the side of the incubator the most extraordinary thing happened. I opened my mouth and said, 'Hello my darling Emma' and her arms and legs went crazy, it was as if she was in an aerobics class! No wonder I used to feel some strong kicks. Roz laughed. 'You know your mama's voice, don't you?' Wow what a moment. I will never forget it.

Roz then proceeded to pick my beautiful girl up, ever so gently and placed her chest on my chest. It was a beautiful sensation. As I was talking, her little fingers were moving and I could even feel her wee nails scratching against my skin.

She kept lifting her head up in response to my voice. I will never forget that day or the feeling of the warmth of her wee body against mine. After having a short cuddle, I was wheeled back to the ward. I felt quite emotional. I needed to ring Bev. I asked the nurse if I could use the phone (these were the days before cell phones). At this stage of my life I had an estranged relationship with my parents, and I needed to share my excitement, and concerns with someone. Bev gave me such calmness and was so down to earth, she was the first of our friends to be introduced to our wee girl.

My wee girl was so small, yet so strong. But I couldn't stop thinking about the spots that covered her wee body. The thing is, Roz didn't mention it or ask me anything about them, when I was having a cuddle. Why I thought, it wasn't as if they weren't obvious. Those small spots made me think of one thing. The virus I had when I had missed my first period. But who was I? I was just the mumma, not a doctor. Roz never mentioned anything about them. Maybe I was worrying about nothing. But my gut was telling me something else. I didn't think it was normal, so what could they possibly be?

It was about two hours later after returning to the ward, that I asked the nurse on duty if I could go back up to NICU to see Emma. 'Of course, you can dear, but don't go tiring yourself out now.' She arranged for an orderly to take me up again.

'Back again?' Roz said. 'Yes,' I replied, 'I just want to look at her in her incubator, I just can't believe she is mine.' That was the truth, but I was also building up the courage to ask Roz what the spots were, except my lips wouldn't work. I opened my mouth, and it was if I had no voice. It couldn't be I was thinking to myself, surely not. She has the measles the voice inside my head was going, just say something!

No it can't be. Stop it Wendy, stop overthinking everything. I must have sat there for another hour until I just blurted the words out.

'Roz? What are those spots covering Emma's body?' There was a pause. 'Umm, we are not sure Wendy.' Oh, my goodness, they are not sure. 'Yes they are proving to be a bit of a puzzle to the doctors as we haven't come across this before. But we will find out, we have taken some blood samples and sent them off to the lab. It is just a matter of waiting for the results,' she said.

I couldn't keep my thoughts to myself anymore. 'Roz,' I said again. She turned to look at me. 'I think I know what those spots are.' She looked deep in thought and at the same time looked confused, saying with her eyes, how could you possibly know what those spots are?

'Say that again Wendy?' she asked. I went on. 'I think I know what those spots are. Emma has the measles or has had the measles.'

'Oh!' she said, 'Just wait there a minute. I need to get a piece of paper and a pen. Can you tell me why you think she has the measles and everything about your pregnancy? Don't leave anything out.'

I started at the beginning, explaining what happened before I became pregnant, when I was sick, and all the concerns I had whilst I was pregnant. Now the doctors had a starting point to go on.

Going home without Emma

It was approximately 10 days after her birth and my scar from the caesarean section was beginning to heal and I wasn't so conscious of knocking that area. To pack my bag and leave the hospital without our first born was not part of the plan. I never want to experience that feeling again. The only thing that kept me going, was that she was in the best hands, and she was born in New Zealand where we had the facilities available to provide her with the care she needed.

Even though we knew we could not take Emma home as there were still a few hurdles to get over, this was still incredibly hard to bear. Her home was the NICU for now. There was not a pregnancy book or 'mum to be book', that prepared you for this journey.

CHAPTER 5

Welcome to the NICU

'I'd rather regret the risks that didn't work out, than the chances I didn't take at all.'
Simone Biles

Our life and time with Emma in the NICU spanned just over three months. It would be an understatement to say that it wasn't an intensive three months.

After explaining my pregnancy journey to the doctors, all sorts of tests were being taken with Emma. I have never seen a baby pricked and prodded with so many needles, either receiving drugs or having blood tests. This was one of the hardest things as a parent to see, especially when they were struggling to find a vein to insert the needle in. They had gone into her arms, legs, feet … but now the head, that just made me cry. It was hard, so very hard, to sit back and allow the professionals to do what they needed to do.

I was fortunate that my employer allowed me to work part-time while Emma was in the baby unit. My days would consist of arriving at the hospital at 7:00 am, staying there for two and half hours, then working from 10:00 am to 2:00 pm, then back to the hospital until 7:30 pm at night.

This was my daily routine, a way of keeping my sanity. If Emma was sleeping, I knitted wee jackets and hats and sewed little nighties for her, as everything else was too big. In between times, I would express my milk, so they could give it to her via tube feeding. I was determined to be the best mum I could be.

Babies that are in the NICU stay in there for many reasons. For some, it is short term stay for a few days, while for others it can be months.

The one thing that made the impossible possible, was the support of the other parents who had babies that were also living in NICU (yes it literally became our home away from home). Even though each baby had their own special medical needs, the one thing we all had in common is that our babies were fragile. You were not alone. In between four hourly care sessions with our babies, we would hang out in the lounge. We would laugh, cry and sometimes just sit there not saying anything at all. We didn't need to. We were all thinking the same thing. Is our baby going to make it.

Being able to talk to each other, or just sit in a comfortable silence, knowing each of us were experiencing the same thoughts, made this journey bearable.

For some parents it was not their first time in NICU due to their family history of previous health conditions. Some of the diagnoses were challenging, or even unknown. This was our case. Emma was a one-off case, and the doctors were just treating her the best way they knew how. There was no textbook that they could go to, to address her condition. The biggest concern that they had, was reducing the stress of her enlarged heart from working so hard.

In the lounge, we had access to many photo albums of previous families and babies that had come through NICU over the years. I called these the 'albums of hope'. When you looked through them, you were presented with photos of very sick babies. Some were on a ventilator, some very undersized and others had various tubes sticking out of them. However, what followed these confronting photos was photos of their progression – photos that they had made it, they survived.

To see these babies two years down the track, running around, playing outside, laughing like any toddler should be doing, was something we could hang on to. We all hoped that would be our child one day.

The NICU Family

It goes without saying, this unit was an intensive place for babies, parents, extended family, nurses, doctors and trainee doctors. Dr Barry Taylor and Dr Roland Broadbent where the presiding specialised doctors looking after the babies in NICU. They were both amazing doctors. Their manner and knowledge had a way of putting you at ease in the most testing and trying situation. I felt so grateful that my daughter was in their care. The number of babies in NICU fluctuated from day to day. At the time Emma was born, there were about 28 babies in the unit, and these babies were placed in one of three sections.

Section 1 was high dependency. All babies in this section, were in stable but critical care. They were either in an incubator, born prematurely, on a ventilator (assisted with breathing) or suffering from another problem that happened either in utero or during childbirth. At one stage there was a 10 pound baby in an incubator next to Emma due to complications during childbirth.

Section 2 was for babies who were stable and out of the incubator and could regulate their body temperature and were not requiring assistance with feeding.

Section 3 (known as the cool room) was for babies who had been consistently feeding, could hold their body temperature, were putting on weight, had come off any medication (or were on very little) and were preparing to go home.

I met some amazing individuals. Mums and dads having their first baby or mums and dads having their second, third or fourth baby. Mums and dads having twins. Sadly, one twin would be doing well, and the other was not.

It was devastating for the parents (and for us) being part of the NICU family to hear the news that one of the babies had died or would not make it out of hospital. We experienced four sets of twins coming through the NICU and the percentage of survival was low. My heart just broke for the parents who were going home with one or no babies. Always knowing that their little one would grow up without their brother or sister that didn't make it.

The time in NICU was a time that I will never forget and the impact it has had on my life is profound. Yes, I would say that this experience was life-changing in more ways than one.

Emma's diagnosis

After 7 weeks, it was discovered that Emma's growth and related health conditions was a result of being exposed to the rubella virus whilst I was pregnant.

Special notes: Measles remains one of the top vaccine-preventable killers of children. Rubella infection in early pregnancy can result in foetal death or birth defects.

Blood cultures grown from blood samples taken from both Emma and I, traced her condition back to this. The rash that covered my body and made me unwell in the early stages of my pregnancy was the measles-rubella virus, known as congenital rubella syndrome (CRS).

In our case, Emma's birth defects resulted in her being growth retarded (small for her age), having an enlarged heart (due to her heart being under stress in utero) and cataract on her eyes (blurry vision – an operation would be able to remove these). The fact that I was exposed to someone with rubella in the very early weeks of pregnancy when all her vital organs were developing meant that her vital organs would be compromised.

On sharing this information with you, I do want to clarify one thing right now that you may all be thinking. If I had known that I had been exposed to the measles when I was pregnant, would I have chosen to have an abortion? The answer would be a categorical no! However, if you asked someone else that question, they may have said yes. We all make decisions based on what we know and what is right for us, regarding our own beliefs and values.

I do not blame our GP for missing this diagnosis – it was a 'blind spot'. Doctors are human as well. They make mistakes, they get things wrong. However, after my experience with this oversight, I am not backwards in coming forward when it comes to the health of myself or my family. As a parent, we know our children better than anyone. Never ignore that feeling you get in 'your gut'. Speak up.

Investigation – why did this happen?

In 1976 there was a change in the administration of the second measles-rubella vaccine. Many slipped through the system.

In 1993, there was a call for all children born between 1963 and 1969 to be checked if they had received their second shot, or if embarking on becoming parents, to get a blood test to see if they had immunity against the measles.

My brain had trouble comprehending this diagnosis and the seriousness of her condition. Because physically to the eye, she looked perfect. She was petite and perfect to me. The enormity of her diagnosis and condition will be imprinted on my mind forever after attending a lecture that I was invited to by the head nurse of NICU, Thea Leveck.

This lecture was held in the Dunedin Public Hospital for doctors and medical students interested in learning about our unique case (specifically on the results of a baby exposed to the rubella virus in utero). Thea asked if it would be okay if I would attend and take questions from the medical staff at the lecture. I agreed.

On entering the lecture theatre doors, I was totally unprepared for the actual size of the auditorium, and the number of doctors in attendance. I couldn't believe so many people were interested in my wee girl. The auditorium was jam-packed. I immediately felt nervous, anxious and very concerned. My mouth started going dry and I could feel myself shaking. I needed to sit down quickly before I fell down. Once I was escorted to a seat with the head nurse, one of the professors opened the session with an introduction of the situation and then said, 'What I am about to show you is an X-ray of her heart.'

There was a collaborative intake of breath from everyone there, including myself. The sound of their 'gasps' went right through me. Even though I didn't understand exactly what I was seeing, I knew that this reaction was not a good sign. The X-ray showed the size of her heart in relation to her chest. It was huge. My mind was racing. I knew at this moment that this was far from normal for any baby.

I felt sick and went numb. I remember being asked a couple of questions by some of the doctors regarding my pregnancy, but by that stage I couldn't even think straight. I felt completely paralysed. This was the first time I had seen this X-ray. As the saying goes, *what has been seen, cannot be unseen.* I can still see the image of her heart even now when I think about it.

On leaving the lecture and returning to the NICU I said to Thea that I was taken aback by the X-ray of Emma's chest and heart. She was completely apologetic and said she would set up a meeting for Neil and I to talk to Dr Roland Broadbent or Dr Barry Taylor.

I began to slowly realise that it was unlikely that Emma was going to be one of those babies in the family room photo album that was going to make it. It didn't matter how much I wanted Emma to live and what she looked like on the outside, it was what was happening on the inside that would determine if she was going to survive.

How could she, with her heart that size, even with all the medication that was being fed into her. It was so hard to take in when she had graduated from her incubator into the second room in her little cot. I thought that was a sign of progress. But was it?

Meeting with the paediatricians

This was a very solemn occasion and an extremely difficult conversation. You don't ever want to hear the words or ask the question, *is my daughter going to live?*

The long and the short of it was, that because Emma's condition was unique, they didn't know if she was going to live for one year or five years. Or if she could live longer. Or if she would always be on oxygen, and whether or not she would be able to take part in physical activities. It was the million-dollar question that no-one had an answer to. From that day onwards, my whole perception of the fragility of her life changed. It was like living with a ticking time bomb. Every minute, every day was so precious. It was the first time I felt completely hopeless. I felt like a tonne of bricks had hit me, and I fell ill.

I was confined to bed with a headache and felt achy all over. For three long days, I could not go to the hospital. The babies in NICU already had their immunity compromised. No-one was allowed to visit unless you were well and presented no risk to babies, parents or nurses.

On returning to the hospital, I was amazed at how much Emma had changed within three days. She looked fuller in the face and much more settled. That cheered me up no end.

Emma continued to put on weight and grow. She was doing well and had graduated from Section 2 to Section 3 of the unit. Surely, it was only a matter a time before we would be taking our wee girl home. It was a great feeling that we were getting a step closer, but also disheartening that progress seemed to have slowed.

Well, one week passed, then two weeks passed and there was still no discussion as to when we would be taking her home. We had been in the NICU for three months. Other babies who had come into Section 3 after Emma had gone home. I just wanted to take my baby home! The problem was that she was still requiring a little bit of oxygen as her saturation levels were low and she also required medication (chlorthalidone) to get rid of excess fluid to reduce stress on her heart. On top of this, she was also having her eyes looked at every two weeks by Dr Peat to ensure that the cataracts were not getting worse.

My positive attitude was waning, and I was beginning to feel tired, depressed and overwhelmed. I put it down to a combination of having full days in the hospital and working part-time. I decided I had better make an appointment with my GP. I told him how I was feeling, and he suggested talking to the doctors to see if there was a possibility of setting a realistic date on when we could take her home.

CHAPTER 6

Precious Little Time

'Don't count the days, make the days count.'
Muhammad Ali

The day had finally arrived! It was 10 days after I saw the GP and Emma now weighed just under 3.5 kg. We were able to take her home. She was still on a small amount of oxygen, and we were allowed to administer her medication ourselves. An appointment was scheduled to bring her back into the hospital in two weeks to have her eyes checked. But it was a fabulous feeling having her home.

The first eye check-up was okay. To ensure that there was no sudden changes with her eyes, she would be reassessed in another two weeks.

My time with Emma at home was so precious. I cuddled her, sang to her, read to her and she loved lying under her mobile, watching the toys swinging around. I also realised that if I put my bright yellow jersey on, she seemed to follow me around the room. Although I wasn't sure if it was her eyes or just the movement of her head that was following me. I would pass this information on to Dr Peat at our next appointment.

18 June 1991 – Four weeks later

It became evident that her cataracts were hindering her ability to see. Dr Peat (the eye specialist) sat down with us and explained what her future would look like, if she were to have this surgery, or not, but also that due to her heart condition, there was a 50 percent chance that she might not survive the surgery. He suggested that we think about it for a couple of days and let him know our decision, so he could make the necessary arrangements. Three days later we confirmed we would go ahead with surgery.

24 June 1991 – Pre-admission

Pre-admission was set for 11:00 am on 24 June 1991, the day before her surgery. Back in the NICU unit, her room was to be the 'isolation room' due to her having contact with the outside world. This was a precautionary measure for the other babies within the unit. She was weighed and was now just over 3.5 kg. Other observations were taken. She was first on the list for surgery the next morning.

It was approximately 7:45 pm that evening, when we finished settling her in the isolation room. Part of me desperately wanted to stay in the 'Parents Room' (near the isolation room) along the corridor, as it was going to be the first night without her Mum or Dad to attend to her feed in the night. However, we were reassured that she would be fine, and we had no reason to believe otherwise.

We were told to go home and enjoy a night of uninterrupted sleep. Reluctantly I did. I insisted that if she became unsettled in the night, that they were to ring me. I didn't care what time it was, just ring. I didn't want her getting worked up before her surgery. This was charted for the nurse who was to take over for the night shift.

I sang Emma her good night song, kissed her head and said to her 'I will see you in the morning darling girl.'

Little did I know that was the last time, I would see my little girl alive.

Numb

The phone call came at 4:05 am Tuesday morning. Neil is hysterical – he took the call. He is saying 'No, no, no, no,' over and over, in between sobs. 'It's okay,' I said, 'you're confused.' It was the first time, I felt that I needed to slap him, to stop him acting so erratically. 'Stop it!' I said.

'Get dressed Wendy, you have to get dressed,' he said. 'We need to go to the hospital. Hurry, we need to go, Emma is dead!'

I got dressed. 'You're not driving,' I said, 'you're in a terrible state.' He insisted. 'No, I am driving. Just get in the car.' There was no point arguing, I just did what I was told and I got in the car.

The hospital was only about seven minutes away from our house, but it seemed like it was taking an eternity to get there. The sooner we get there the better, I kept saying to myself. This is a mistake, there has been a mistake, we are going to look like fools arriving at the hospital at this time in the morning. This is nothing but a bad nightmare. This is all wrong. Neil is horribly confused.

Why Me?

We pulled up outside the hospital in the five-minute park. I got out of the car and reached for Neil's hand. He held my hand and squeezed it. I remember half walking, half running to the lift to take us to Level 5 of the hospital where NICU was located. We had to run pass security, but the security guy knew our faces from previous visits to the hospital. You get to know a lot of people in the hospital when you've been there for nearly three and half months.

We jumped in the lift pushed the button for Level 5. 'Ting' went the bell as the lift doors opened. We ran down the first part of the hallway until you get to the path where you have the option to go left or right. Turning left takes you to the NICU unit. Then you have to enter two sets of doors before you gain access to the NICU unit. As we approached the first set of doors (the fire doors), I could see two doctors standing side on through the portal window. They were there, ready to meet us. Ready and waiting. Yes, they were expecting us.

Now Neil's nightmare was becoming my nightmare. No! No! No! voices were screaming inside my head. No, no, no. This is not some nightmare; this is really happening. Someone, please just wake me up, please someone. But no-one would because it was real.

As I walked towards the doors, their heads turned, and I could see their faces through the windows in the doors. There it was, the look, the expression – the look of sadness and hopelessness. They opened the doors, and we were greeted with the words, 'We are so sorry.'

Goodbye Emma

She lay in her cot, and she looked different. The oxygen tube that had been part of her wee face that was secured above her lip and under her nose had been removed. Why had they removed it? Of course, she didn't need it. She lay there as if she was asleep – with her whole body in tack.

I touched her face, the voices inside my head were screaming inside, *Please Emma, please open your eyes, please just open your eyes! Mummy is here. I am so sorry for leaving you, I am here now, please just wake up.*

I just wanted to see her blue eyes, there was so much life and brightness in them. I took one of her little hands in my finger. She was perfect in every way. I picked her up to cradle her. Her body was still warm, it was just so hard to comprehend, that this wee baby who only hours ago was smiling, flapping her arms, making go-ga noises was gone. She was completely lifeless.

As I held her, I began to feel angry. I started firing many questions at the doctors. What happened? How could this go so wrong? She wasn't supposed to die in the hospital! She was in the safest place she could be! And she hadn't even had her operation yet!

Out of this devastation, I was trying to make some sort of sense out of the whole situation. I wasn't prepared for this. How am I supposed to function? What do I do now? My whole world was tipped upside down and inside out. I was in shock. I was numb.

The doctor in charge proceeded to tell me that the nurse who had been assigned to looking after Emma, had gone on a tea break, and on returning from her tea break, she found Emma covered in vomit. The nurse had no clue what had happened. As Emma was in the isolation room, no other nurse would have been watching her.

Prior to the nurse going on her tea break, she had checked on Emma, and although she was a bit unsettled, her observations were fine. The doctors worked on Emma for over 30 minutes to bring her back. But nothing worked.

When the nurse found Emma, it could not be determined if she had died due to choking on her vomit or if her heart had gone into an irregular heart rhythm and it was her body's way of shocking itself (through vomiting) to get the heart back into a regular rhythm.

I thought I was going to pass out. This was about all I could take. It was going to require an autopsy to confirm the cause of death. I could not bear the thought of her dying by choking on her own vomit! It was incomprehensible that 'she' a little fighter and 'we' had been through so much for her life to end from choking on her own vomit. I then immediately transitioned from a state of disbelief to anger and guilt. Angry with myself for leaving my daughter on her own in the hospital and the guilt in my mind that this could have been avoidable. Why did I leave her by herself? I should have stayed. She wouldn't have died if I had stayed. It was all too much.

I had to ring someone. I needed to talk to my dad. I had only started to reconnect with my parents after finding out I was going to have a premature baby. I felt that whatever happened between us, was between us, but that they had a choice if they wanted to be involved in their granddaughter's life. They had a right to know and so did Emma.

I was torn to ring him or not. Should I wait until it was a more sociable hour or just phone him? It was approximately 5:30 am by this time. I knew that when he looked at the clock before he answered he would either know that someone had died, or if it was a phone call from Scotland. I was born in Scotland and my parents immigrated to New Zealand when I was eight months old. As the majority of Mum and Dad's family were still in Scotland, it wasn't unusual to get phone calls at ungodly hours of the morning from friends who may have been out for a few bevies (which is another word for getting drunk) and decided to ring New Zealand and have a chat with Jock, or from family, eager to share some news, or that an old schoolmate had died. Growing up it was a standard joke, but this time it wasn't funny. This time it was me giving the bad news, and news that I couldn't comprehend myself.

The phone seemed to ring and ring forever. Just to put you in the picture, this was the era of the old landline where the telephone was based in the hallway or lounge before it was normal to have cell phones by the bed. At last Dad answered the phone in a crackly half-asleep Scottish voice. 'Hello?' he said. 'Dad, Dad, Dad …' I was sobbing, I couldn't get the words out. 'Dad, Emma is dead!'

'What!' he replied. 'Dad Emma is dead, can you please come into the unit I feel sick.'

'Oh no,' he cried, 'I am on my way.' I waited for my dad to arrive, which felt like an eternity. For a moment I felt as if I had regressed to my four-year-old self. This was a terrible nightmare. I was sure that I would wake up any minute and it would all be okay. Dad would make it okay.

As a child, if I had a nightmare, I would tiptoe into Mum and Dads' room (the only time I was allowed) and tap Dad on the shoulder and whisper, 'Dad, I need a cuddle, I have had a scary dream.' I would never go around to Mum's side of the bed, because if you chanced your luck you would be greeted by a rottweiler dog, (you learnt never to wake the Mumma) but Dad would always let you snuggle in for a few minutes, reassuring me that it was a bad dream, before telling me to pop off back into my own bed. But this time, he couldn't make it right. He could only hold me as I sobbed my heart out.

The nurses and doctors did their best to support us, to say the right things. Some did and some did not.

News soon reached Dr Peat the eye specialist who was to perform surgery on Emma at 7:30 am and he was advised that she had died in the night. He came up to the NICU unit to offer his condolences. The pain on his face was genuine, he was a dad as well. I am glad for both their sakes that Emma did not die during the operation.

CHAPTER 7

A Foreign Path

'I know that the ones that love you will miss you.'
Keanu Reeves

Calling the funeral director to organise your child's funeral is something a parent never ever wants to do. EVER. It is the hardest thing I have ever had to do in my entire life.

It's not right! No child is supposed to die before their parents.

I don't know how long we sat in the isolation room with her, taking turns holding her and facing the fact she wasn't going to wake up. We agreed for an autopsy to be carried out. Once this had been undertaken her wee body would be released to the funeral home. We had to ring the funeral home to advise them that our daughter had died and to make arrangements for them to collect her from the mortuary. Even to this day as I pen these words, this memory puts my stomach in a knot. It still makes we feel queasy.

The thing is, I didn't know of any funeral homes. I had only attended one funeral. It was my cousin's grandfather which was held at the crematorium, and it was awful. It was so cold and morbid. This was new territory, and I didn't know what to do. Dr Taylor spoke softly to the two of us and told us we will need to ring one of the funeral homes. There was no right or wrong one, you just had to pick one. But who was going to make the call? Neil looked at me and I looked at him. 'I can't,' he said, 'I just can't!' My brain just couldn't think. I didn't even know where to start. 'Would you like me to get the telephone directory for you?' asked Dr Taylor. 'Yes,' I said, 'thank you.' Thank you? Thank you for what? Goodness, was I even having this conversation? He exited the room and returned with the telephone directory.

I just went into robot mode. All I remember is ringing 'Hope and Sons' saying my name, that my baby girl had died, and were they able to take care of the arrangements. I don't even, know how I managed to get the words out. It felt like they were being said by another person. It just wasn't real. The rest is a blur.

Emma at home before the funeral

As I am writing this part of my story, I can picture this day so very clearly. Before I continue, I just want to acknowledge how caring and sensitive our funeral directors, Hope and Sons in Dunedin were. They made the unbearable bearable. We were contacted ahead of time, before Emma was returned home, so we would not be sitting around wondering and waiting. She was returned to us in the most adorable, beautiful white casket. I feel the tears welling up as I write this. She was placed in the middle of her bedroom. Neil and I braced ourselves. Her casket was delicately placed on a stand and the top of the casket removed.

She just looked like a little doll.

We had many friends and family visit us over the next two days before her funeral. We were so grateful for the love, aroha, kindness and support, and food given, but all I wanted to do was use every minute I possibly had to just sit and talk to Emma. I was aware I only had so many minutes before she was gone, physically that is, again. I wish I could just stop time. It just felt so unfair.

The post-mortem results

It was confirmed that Emma's heart had gone into an irregular rhythm and that it was the heart's way of getting it back into a regular rhythm by making the body vomit. In some ways this news was a relief. I could not have accepted another answer. The thought that it could have been a preventable death, especially while in a hospital, would have been too much to bear.

The day of the funeral

For a wee person who had such a short life, the turnout to her funeral was massive. My heart was overwhelmed by the love, care and support from everyone that attended. There were friends I had grown up with, my work mates, the new families I had met in the hospital along with their babies and children, neighbours and friends of neighbours. It brought me great comfort for the mums and dads that I had meet in the unit to bring their babies. I didn't think for a minute that life was unfair that they had their baby, and I didn't have mine, rather it was Emma's little friends coming to say goodbye and understanding that anyone of us could have been having a funeral for our child. We 'knew' first hand, how fragile life was. It was facing the 'uncomfortableness' of the situation that brought comfort.

I didn't know until the morning of the funeral if I would be able to get up and speak about her short life or not. I did. I don't know where the courage or desire came from, but I had an overwhelming urge and need to share our story with those attending. I just wanted everyone that was present to know how precious she was to us, and the impact she had on our lives. If there wasn't a dry eye in the house by the time I had finished my eulogy, there certainly wasn't when we played her farewell song by Joe Cocker 'You are so beautiful'. The words described everything we both felt.

Neil carried her wee casket out to the hearse, that was heartbreaking. Emma was cremated. We could not bear the thought of her being in a graveyard all by herself. It did take us a few months to collect her ashes. Neil finally had the courage to do it. I guess for me, it was accepting that she was gone, and I couldn't do it. I wasn't mentally 'there yet'. This is the one thing about grief, we all deal with it differently and we move through emotions all in our own time. There is no right or wrong time, it is having the patience with each other to understand this. We brought a beautiful yellow miniature rose that was put in a pot outside the kitchen that held her ashes. She would be near us, and if we decided to move house, we could take her with us.

CHAPTER 8

Broken-hearted

*'It is a pity to shoot the pianist
when the piano is out of tune.
The Piano is badly out of tune, when your life is in disarray, and you lose the person that you love. But throwing away or wasting the life that is left, is a classic way of shooting the pianist.
Be kind to yourself and give yourself time.
Remember even the most out of tune pianos can be made to play good music again.'*

Rene Coty

I didn't sleep much after Emma was gone, and when I did, it was because I had cried myself to sleep. We were fortunate to have employers who gave us special extended leave. We were both a mess, physically and mentally, so it was much appreciated.

I felt like the saddest person on the planet. To be perfectly honest, I would pray to God, to take me in the night so I didn't have to wake up in the morning. 'Jehovah,' I screamed inside 'just take me, put me out of my misery!'. What was I going to live for? What did I have to live for? It really was so difficult to imagine how life could be better or different from the emptiness I was experiencing. At one point, I thought God was going to answer my prayer, to just slip away in my sleep, as I developed a profound pain in my heart. The pain felt as if someone had reached inside my body and was squeezing my heart with all their might. *Squeeze harder* I would say to myself, *just make it end*. This pain continued for a few days. I decided I had better make an appointment with our GP as I was still having trouble going to sleep, and if I was to function, and be of any assistance at work, I needed some help.

The doctor explained that the medical term I was suffering from regarding the pain in my heart was takotsubo cardiomyopathy, also known as broken-heart syndrome. He said this was a temporary heart condition that can be brought on by sudden or extreme forms of emotional stress such as grief. The symptoms mimic a heart attack. He reassured me that I would not die from it as I was a young, fit, healthy person and it should pass in time. This pain lasted between four and five months. I was also prescribed sleeping tablets for the first few weeks, but had to return for another two weeks supply, until finally I was able to fall asleep without crying myself to sleep.

Grief support

Returning to work was tough. It was tough in two ways. One, when I looked into my colleagues faces, I could see in their eyes my pain and their pain as a parent. It was that look, *How can you do it? I can't even imagine what you have gone through*. And two, I had a great job, but this was not what I wanted to be doing. I just wanted to be a mum, at home with my baby.

There were two support groups that we were aware of for bereaved parents. One was the 'cot death' group. This was when your baby died unexpectedly in their sleep for no rhyme or reason.

Then there was another group that meet occasionally for parents that had lost a grown child, either through, illness, accident or suicide. To be fair, I could barely cope with my own grief, that I just couldn't bear the pain of anyone else. I just wanted someone who could hold my hand, just hold me to comfort me. To not ask questions, to not tell me it was going to be okay, or that I would soon get over it. Each time someone made that last comment, I literally had to sit on my hands as I thought I would punch them in the face.

My mind often thought of how the other mums and bubs were doing that I had met in the hospital. The ones that had gone home before us and the ones that were still in there after we came home. It was a very unique and special place. Everyone knew just how fragile life was without saying it.

I will never forget the phone call I received from Sue a few weeks after Emma's death. She phoned and told me that she had previously been in the baby unit with one of her other pregnancies and the baby didn't make it. She knew how I felt. *'It was tough, it was a lonely place to be, and it really hurt. The pain doesn't go away, but you learn to live with it,'* she said. It was so good to have my feelings validated.

Just hearing those words at the time was a godsend. She helped me realise that I wasn't going mad. It made a huge difference. It didn't stop my sadness, but It was such a reassuring feeling to be understood.

The guilt

To think back and figure out how I managed to survive the first year after Emma's death is a bit of a miracle. I was deeply affected, mentally and physically. To just get through the day took so much effort. Leaving Emma in the hospital by herself (the night before her surgery) left me riddled with guilt. It was the 'what if' thoughts going through my mind. What if I had stayed, maybe she wouldn't have become unsettled and distressed and her heart wouldn't have got into an irregular heartbeat and she would still be alive. As a mother I 'felt' that I had abandoned her. How could I have done this? I blamed myself for her death. Why? Because on top of leaving her in the hospital by herself, the blood cultures taken from me, when I was in the hospital with Emma, showed that I hadn't received my full vaccination as a child for the measles! If I had done, she wouldn't have suffered in this way. The blaming game began. And so did the nightmares.

The nightmares

They may have started differently, but they always ended the same. I would be out walking with Emma in her pram. I would stop and talk to someone in the park, then look down into the pram, and she was gone. Someone had taken her! Or in another dream, a friend had come over to look after her while I popped out to the supermarket, and on arriving home my friend would be distraught saying that someone had abducted her whilst I was out. It was awful. Every dream ended the same, with her gone.

I always woke up distressed and crying. I felt sick most of the time and didn't feel like eating. To stop the nightmares, I found myself drinking to numb the pain or to conk out (fall asleep). I realised a habit was forming, but it was the only way I seemed to cope, with my new reality. The hardest part of the week was the weekend, getting used the deathly silence that now occupied our home.

As a couple and as time progressed, we found that we went from hugging each other to nothing. We couldn't talk, we couldn't comfort each other, we were just so lost and felt like we were getting more and more distant from each other. It wasn't a matter of should we think about trying for another baby, it was more like, are we going to make it as a couple? We both seemed to be living in 'this trance'. For me, it was a weird feeling. I felt like I was in this glass box; I could see out, people could see in, but there was nothingness. I couldn't hear or speak. They could see me, but not hear me. I was only there in body. I felt dead, and I was functioning like a robot would. Black and blue were now my favourite colours. Colour to me meant life, joy and happiness. That was gone. When or if I would feel those emotions again, that was the million-dollar question.

The truth of the matter is that we couldn't help each other emotionally. We were trying to understand our own pain, that we couldn't comfort each other emotionally. At the time I felt guilty about this, that I was a failure as a wife somehow. However, I found out further down the track, that it is not uncommon for couples to separate after the death of a child, because they find it so hard to communicate how they are feeling. There is just so much pain.

Each time we looked into each other's eyes, there was this incredibly sad person looking back at you and it was a constant reminder that a part of you and a part of them had died.

Most of our friends hadn't started their family yet, so they had no idea what to say, or do, to help us. They were struggling with the concept of, 'What if this happens to us when we decide to have a baby?'

Why is it so hard to accept death?

Have you ever wondered why someone will fight for their life until the end, or why it is sad to see anyone we love die, no matter what age they are? Because God created us with eternity in our heart. No-one is looking forward to death. It is not in us. The exception being if you are suffering in some way and have been for a long time.

> 'He hath made everything beautiful in its time:
> also he hath set eternity in their heart...'
> Ecclesiastes 3:11, American Standard Bible
> (abridged)

It was never his purpose for us to die. That is why it hurts so much to lose a loved one.

CHAPTER 9

My Aching Arms

'Trauma is not just a story or an experience, but it is physical changes that happen in the brain.'
Dr Bessel van der Kolk

My arms just ache, when will this feeling leave me? I keep telling my mind that there is no baby to pick up or hold, but equally I am longing to hold her again.

For now, the numbness has lifted, and new emotions of anger and sadness have entered my mind and body. I feel tortured when I watch the news and hear of babies and children neglected or hurt by their parents. It just isn't right. I would give anything just to have Emma back in my arms. I have all this love to give but no-one to give it to.

I was desperately trying to reconcile why I felt so empty, sad and alone. Then, I finally figured it out: it was the first time that I felt love, actually 'felt love' and could give love. It was a completely new emotion for me. I felt alive! Emma had awakened something within me.

You see for me growing up in a very strict religious household 'love' meant discipline, but it was harsh discipline. Affection or praise was rarely displayed. It was always punishment first, then ask questions later. Saying 'no' or talking back (even when I was trying to explain that 'I didn't do it! It wasn't me!'), resulted in a harder or more severe punishment. It was not allowed. It was classed as being defiant, disrespectful or disobedient.

The world I was brought up in, was seen as good or bad, or black or white, or it was right or wrong. There was no in-between, no grey areas, no tolerance for any other view or mistakes. It was a rigid way to live. I was constantly on high alert, waiting to be scolded or smacked for the next thing I did wrong. I was a child trying to learn and grow, of course I was going to make mistakes.

I had trouble reconciling how this type of parenting reflected the example of Jesus that we were constantly reminded to imitate at our congregation. Everything I knew and read about Jesus, was that he was kind, tolerant, patient and understanding. This was not what I experienced. For me it was like walking on eggshells most of the time. Waiting to be punished for the next thing I did wrong.

I was told to obey any authority, teachers, police officers, elders, any adult, because they are an 'adult'. So, I grew up thinking that 'I didn't matter' and my 'needs' didn't matter. I didn't know what it meant to have boundaries, or to be able to say no without feeling guilty. (That is why I felt so uncomfortable questioning the nurse about Emma's spots. The voice inside my head was saying, 'Who do you think you are to question someone in this position?').

It was acceptable practice back then for any adult to strap, belt, slap, pinch or use 'reasonable force' on a child that left you with welts, bruises or marks. Research over the past 50 years has shown that this type of punishment, although well intended, has had a huge physical and psychological effect on many adults, including myself.

Children, therapists and doctors would now call it cruel and abusive. Abuse, that kills the soul of the child. Many parents and my parents just weren't emotionally available, they were tuned into us physically, but not emotionally. They didn't have their own emotional needs meet by their parents. Most parents of this era were emotionally retarded, for example, how many times were you told to 'stop your crying' or I'll give you something to cry about', or 'don't you raise your voice to me!' When those words are constantly repeated, it wears you down and makes you feel ashamed and worthless for who you are.

Dr Bruce Perry a renowned brain development and trauma expert discusses this in his book, *What Happened to You?*:

'A cold, disengaged, partially attentive caregiver can have immediate, and potentially lifelong toxic effects on the developing child. This child may grow up feeling inadequate, and unlovable. Even with many gifts and skills, they will feel that they are not enough as an adult, and that can lead to a host of maladaptive behaviours including unhealthy forms of attention seeking, self-sabotage or even self-destructive behaviour'.

The consequence is, there are many adults living with a wounded inner child.

This type of parenting style was from an era of patriarchal parenting that many parents implemented, modelled off their own parents, then adapted to what they wanted to implement or dump.

John Bradshaw, therapist and author, explains this 'parenting style' in his book *Homecoming*:

> *'Patriarchy is characterised by male dominance (but it doesn't mean that only men do it though), woman raised by a patriarch can become a patriarch. It is based on blind obedience, obedience without context, "you do it because I said so!" A lot of parents acted "shameless" by acting like they "know it all". It is based on the repression of all emotions, except fear. It is based on the crushing of the will at an early age, that is "you obey me".'*

I craved love, and the only way that I felt I could be loved was by thinking and doing what my parents required from me as a child. My purpose and identity in life was to take care of others and make sure that they were okay before anything else. It was classed as being 'selfish' to ask for anything. To feel any sense of self-worth, others needs always came first before my own.

To be a people pleaser at all costs. I unconsciously developed a 'false self', or 'a mask' because in that way I found a way 'to matter'. In her book *The Ultimate You*, Sharon Pearson describes this false self in detail. It is what we do as a child to survive, because who else would look after us? We can't take care of ourselves! I just learnt to shut down, be compliant or numb out.

The best statement I have heard describing what I felt was by Joel Colbert in John Bradshaw's book *Creating Love*: 'I was most loveable when I was not being me.'

Many religious preachers teach that the highest form of love is self-sacrifice, to set aside one's own physical, emotional and intellectual needs to serve and take care of others. They teach long suffering and martyrdom as two of the major ways to attain goodness. 'Acting good' and 'acting righteous' were more important than actually being good. 'Acting loving' was more important than 'being loving'. For many years I believed that this was how every Christian person behaved, and that this was the right way to be, to get approval or to get love. This is wrong; the Bible even says that we need to take care of ourselves.

My parents were children of the war, and sometimes they experienced a lack of food, clothing, or the absence of coal to heat the house. So, it was no wonder, they became angry, when we spilt the milk or broke a plate when we were drying the dishes. The thing is, as a child I never set out to do this intentionally, but you were punished as if you did. That's what hurt the most.

It is tough being a parent and I understand that they were parenting us the best way they knew how. They also had their own emotional struggles to deal with that I wasn't aware of until my mid-twenties. My dad's mum lived in Scotland twelve thousand miles away and suffered from severe mental illness and depression. He would get homesick, and on top of that my parents were always watching their pennys. Dad had many responsibilities as an elder in our congregation. This position meant there was a lot of pressure to be an 'exemplary example' which required that his children be a 'fine example'. To achieve this result, he needed us to be kept on the straight and narrow which required severe discipline. There was no reasoning or a loving explanation about what you did or didn't do wrong. It was discipline first, then ask questions later. I used to think that God must think I am very bad person to get those wallops, smacks, skelps or whatever you want to call it. I know now through my studies that a person 'can't give what they don't have'. Dad didn't have a mother who was emotionally present because of her illness, so in his mind he thought he was being a good parent. It wasn't right, but it is an explanation of why I was raised the way I was. I see them through a different lens now, they weren't bad people, their behaviour was bad.

What I am grateful for is the time my mum gave me to teach me the skills of how to be a capable wife. My mum was a great cook, dressmaker, knitter and homemaker. She spent every season preparing jams, pickles and preserves from the garden. She shared all these wonderful skills with me. It was reassuring to know that I was good at something.

However, I really struggled emotionally as a teenager. By the time I was 14 years old, my home life became stricter, and it was hard to reason with my dad. So, when I was 17 and a boy came along and told me that he 'loved me' I thought that was the most wonderful thing in the world, because I thought I was unlovable. I loved him for being able to love me. I know that sounds really messed up, but as Dr Bruce Perry, in his book *What Happened to You?* explains: *'Dismissive caregiving can lead to an unquenchable thirst for love. You cannot love if you have not been loved'*.

But there was another problem to contend with. Neil wasn't of the same faith as me and that was a big no-no in our family. So I was given the ultimatum to stop seeing him or move out of home. That was the rules. I was so desperately unhappy, I chose the latter. I was done, physically, mentally and emotionally.

I just remember saying to myself, 'I surrender, I've had enough, I just don't want to feel like this any longer,' just very sad and empty. Equally I felt so low and numb, like a child who had been abandoned by her parents, the very ones that are supposed to protect you and love you. So, between 17 and 25 years of age, I only saw my parents about four times. It was only due to being admitted to the hospital that we reconnected.

My Aching Arms

So when she died, I felt like my 'whole' world had fallen apart.

At 25 years of age, it was very hard to envisage how the future was supposed to look brighter or get better. There were some pretty dark days, and yes suicide crossed my mind, but I was aware enough then to know I would just be transmitting my wounds and pain onto my parents and my friends. The reality was, I didn't want to die. I just wanted the physical and mental pain to stop.

CHAPTER 10

Grief and Surviving the First Year

'Understanding why you are messed up, doesn't stop you from being messed up!'
Dr Bessel van der Kolk

I remember, saying to my husband, what on earth did we do with our days before Emma arrived? We thought we had a fulfilling life before she entered our world, but we had no idea of the love that was to fill our hearts. No-one can describe what happens at the birth of a child, you suddenly feel whole as a person and a couple. You both look at each other, with your eyes saying, *look what we made, she is a little bit of me and a little bit of you*. The feeling is almost euphoric. But when that life ends, the closeness you felt as a couple seems a million miles away.

Before leaving the hospital that day, the day Emma died, I was handed a pamphlet about grief by the hospital's social worker. An A4 piece of paper, 'The Steps of Grief', that was to get us through this misery. Excuse my sarcasm but, it was like sending you home with a Band-Aid on an open surgical wound on your head. There was so much wrong about the whole situation. We were not dealing with a cut finger here; we were two young, traumatised parents trying to understand the enormity of what had just happened to us. The social worker isn't to blame, that was what was available at the time, 32 years ago. I want to change that now! Why? Because what I know now about grief, trauma, the brain and our emotions, could have saved years of silence and internal torment. My mind can only wonder how the mothers and fathers managed in the first and second world wars, when their sons never returned home. In fact, if I can be so bold and answer that question myself: they didn't! All I know is that their pain has been passed down through the generations. It is no wonder, many drank themselves into oblivion to stop the hurt, or committed suicide.

The question is, how can you heal if you don't know the beast you are dealing with? Or have someone to guide you through it? It is a trauma.

Trauma wasn't even a thing until about 20 years ago, let alone considered a factor in a person's health. I can only thank the doctors who have made it their life's work to find out more about the human condition; such as Dr Bruce Perry and Dr Bessel van der Kolk. I feel a sadness in my heart when I think of my dad's mum, who also experienced the loss of two of her children and what she went through. Her second child Alex died of silent pneumonia in his sleep when he was three years old and her youngest son, my Uncle Danny took his life at the 23 years of age. How she must have suffered. She was in and out of hospital over the years with depression. When I was 20 I did my big OE to meet all my relatives in Scotland. My Grandmother was in hospital and I wanted to meet her in person. My Aunty Peggy (Dad's older sister) took me in to see her. Growing up in Dunedin, I had only seen two photos of my Grandmother. One when she was a young girl, and one of her in Mum and Dad's wedding photo. When I visited her, what I saw shocked me to the core. She was incredibly agitated and was surrounded by dribbling, doped up patients and there was this peculiar smell that permeated the room. I wanted to leave. I thought I was going to throw up. I was not prepared for this at all. It was so confronting for a young 20-year-old. So, when I was feeling all over the place with my emotions, after Emma died, I was too scared to tell anyone for fear I would end up in the same predicament. I would rather just 'exist' then end up in an institution such as that.

In the words of trauma researcher and author Dr Bessel van der Kolk:

'Being traumatised is not just an issue of being stuck in the past, it is just as much of a problem of not being fully alive in the present.'

Describing How Grief – Your Trauma – Changes You

A dear friend asked me one day, many years later, how would you describe the effects of losing your child? I sat there and thought about that question for a few seconds. I really couldn't put it into one or two words, because you cannot erase from your mind what has happened, so I used this analogy:

> *Have you had sex, and do you enjoy it? Now I want you to imagine your life before you had sex or made love. Just try ... can you?*
>
> *How would you explain to someone who hasn't had sex, what it is like so that they could imagine walking in your shoes to feel what you feel? It's tricky isn't it? Why? Because it is a*

mental, emotional and physical change in your 'whole' body not just part of you – it is all of you. All of you is affected. You are moved by the sight of the person, the touch of the person, the smell of the person, the firmness of their butt or the softness of their breasts, the taste of their lips, the sound of their breath changing from anticipation, the closeness of your bodies against each other, the thoughts you are thinking of what you are about to feel and enjoy and the arousal in your loins, that soon you will be carried away with the enjoyment and intensity of the act, then reaching orgasm.

All of your senses are involved. It is life-changing!

So can you go back, and recall life as it was, before experiencing the feeling of sex? You can't. You can't go back and imagine it being otherwise, can you?

Validation and Understanding

My wish for you is that from this day forward, you never feel alone again or feel as if there is something wrong with you. Anything on the following list, is a normal reaction for what you are going through.

- Feeling depressed (if you start feeling suicidal tell someone you can trust straight away or contact your doctor. If you have started planning your suicide, you need to ring 111 (for New Zealand) or go to the Emergency Department IMMEDIATELY!) See the back of the book for different health agencies and help lines
- Shock, denial, numb, depressed, anger, sadness and GUILT
- Dismissing that it happened – you 'know it' but won't 'accept it'

- Resentment
- Loneliness – there is no one to talk to who understands the same pain
- Foggy brain
- No motivation
- Feeling utter exhaustion for months
- Nightmares – different scenarios playing out through your mind, but each nightmare ending the same way – your loved one has been taken, killed, or is lost
- Feeling distant from friends and family
- Receiving judgement and criticism from others – you are told that you 'shouldn't be feeling this way'; 'you should be over it' or you 'should have moved on by now', or you need to 'pray harder'
- Torturing yourself with the what-ifs?
- Wearing black all the time – you just want to stay hidden
- Feeling anxious about being on your own
- Socially withdrawn
- Looking and feeling dishevelled
- Feeling completely hopeless
- Blame of self or others
- Play depressing music not to feel better but to feel worse
- Fear of visiting hospitals or funeral homes
- Drinking excessively
- Screaming
- You start swearing (cussing) constantly which you never did previously
- You want to hide under the bed covers and never come out
- To get out of bed in the morning, you have to just make yourself 'do it' because if you thought about it, you would never get up
- You feel as if your partner does not understand your pain
- You wonder if your relationship with your partner will survive

- You fight or withdraw from your partner
- Your dreams have been shattered – you feel despondent
- Scared you will bump into someone who doesn't know that your child has died, and hear the dreaded question? How is your ... you know what I mean
- Feeling anxious when attending parties, dinners, weddings and other special events, or trying to avoid attending these events
- Trying to be happy when you feel so sad. Fear of being put in a psychiatric unit for disclosing what you are honestly feeling
- You want to die, and can't see how things would ever be better again

Triggers

- Hearing people use your child's name
- Hearing babies cry at the supermarket
- Hearing songs that remind you of your loved one
- Anniversaries of any kind that intensify your sadness
- Your child's birthdate
- Walking past their bedroom and they aren't there
- Visiting your child's grave site (or it could have the opposite effect). There is no right or wrong way.

It is messy, but it is normal. Don't expect too much of yourself. Your body and mind are trying to make sense of your new world.

You are dealing with a Trauma

As Dr Bessel van der Kolk explains, 'Trauma robs you of the feeling that you are in charge of yourself'. So, this is a time to be kind and compassionate to yourself.

> *You must give yourself permission*
> *to treat yourself with compassion.*
> *Your body and mind are in shock.*
> *(See Part 2: Brain and Trauma)*

Try this on for size:

Imagine if you have just been told that your friend has been in a severe car accident. The impact was such that they needed to be cut from the wreckage, they barely escaped with their life. Every bone in their body was broken and they have a severe head injury. They have been put into an induced coma and will spend a minimum of six months in the hospital before they can go home, and will require further outpatient follow-ups, medical care and surgery.

Would you expect them to be the same person physically or mentally as they were before the accident? Or would you tell them to stop having a pity party, because they couldn't do the things they could before the accident? No, of course not.

You need people around you that can support you and have your back, that will encourage you to speak freely about how you feel.

Go crazy and write your own kind of messy on the next page. If all you can muster up is a scribble or a four letter word, let it out.

IT'S MESSY

CHAPTER 11

Needs as a Couple

*'We don't need to be alone –
we just need to know how to connect.'*
Wendy B King

You will be feeling different emotions at different times, as each of you have your own unique ways of processing your thoughts and emotions. As the man, your way of receiving comfort may be through intimacy, yet as a woman, that may be the last thing on your mind. This can be interpreted by the man as 'you don't care about me', and as for the woman, 'are you crazy, you are so selfish, always thinking about sex!'. It's complicated. This is why you need extra help to get through this. There is also the possibility your extended family is struggling as well.

Having an independent person who is not closely connected to your loss, or seeing a therapist or grief counsellor, may definitely help. Why? For some of us, we were not allowed to express our emotions, so we can become stuck in not knowing how 'to be'. However, for it to be a good experience you need to feel safe and feel understood, and that you are not just another number. Just talking about your experience will not help, you need a combination of feeling work and strategies to assist you in your mental and emotional wellbeing. Ideally the person you are seeing has some knowledge or experience of what you are going through. Not all therapists or coaches are the same. Do not be put off by having a bad experience with one therapist or coach. Any relationship requires trust. In Part 2 you will find tips to help you search for the right person for you. We need to feel understood, but we also need a sense of connection and belonging, to a community or group where we can have fun, sing, dance, or explore nature in. Connection is vital, as isolation eats away at your soul.

Your Emotions

Do not be afraid of your feelings or emotions! Part 2 goes into more depth about 'Why?'.

In Remi (Sharon) Pearson's book *Ultimate You*, her research shows that there are 'No negative emotions'. She explains:

'All emotions have their place within you, and all emotions are valid. To avoid some of them, because they are "too negative" is to avoid aspects of yourself.' (People confuse feelings with 'acting out' – that is a behaviour.)

I learnt to have feelings without being disabled by them. This only happens when you 'learn' how to feel your emotions. One of the biggest mistakes as a human race is being fearful of our emotions. We have been conditioned to be shamed for who we are.

These emotions are biologically designed to be felt and leave the body. They are part of our physiology. Dr Bruce Perry shares another important fact in his book, *What Happened to You?:* 'Our brain is organised to act and feel before we think. This is how our brain develops; sequentially from the bottom up.'

From Denial to Acceptance

The major requirement for the journey is a willingness to let go of the 'attachment' to your current experience of life.

The biggest challenge is accepting the death of your child. It feels so final. It is so painful, that you want to push it away, out of your mind. You 'know' that it has happened, but you don't want to 'accept that it happened'. I struggled with this for years. I had an internal warfare going on in my mind. I was trying to reason with my thoughts on why it shouldn't have happened to me, and 'if only' things could have been different. Literally, *Why ME?* In fact, my password for everything was the word 'hopeless' because, one I wouldn't forget it and two, it was how I felt. But there was also another part to this that was buried deep inside that I didn't unravel for years and that was my expectation of being a mumma. My plan in my head of how my life 'should' have turned out was ripped away from me. I was angry because 'this wasn't supposed to happen to me. Why me? I was a good person. I failed to realise in my young mind, that being a good person has nothing to do with Emma dying. It was the disappointment and expectation in my head of how I thought things should have played out in my life, but they didn't.

Apart from the phone call to Dad telling him that 'Emma was dead'– (the words didn't really register. I was in shock and it didn't feel real). I couldn't bring myself after that occasion, to say the words again out loud. I thought that if I did, it would make everything about her disappear and I didn't want her memory or anything about her to fade. This was 'my new reality' and I couldn't deal with it for a very long time.

But here is the thing; until we acknowledge the pain, and embrace it, or invite the pain in, we cannot heal or begin to move forward if we keep avoiding it. I know this sounds odd, but it is true. I had to do this work myself. In fact the opposite happens, you have such a release of tension and anxiety that you feel lighter. Your memory of them does not fade, and when you think about them, the intensity of loss has lifted.

You may or may not be able to do or say this right now, as it is confronting, but I want you to consider coming back to this section to do this exercise or have a friend hold your hand or just be with you or close by when you have the courage to do it. So, when you are ready, I want you to put your left hand or right hand on your heart, close your eyes and take a big breath, and another big breath. Then out loud I want you to say the name of your child out loud 'is dead'. I will say it with you: 'Emma is dead'.

The reason why you need to say it out loud, is that it makes it real. How many times, have you been thinking about something that stirs feelings within you, but it is not until you say it out loud, that you get all choked up or start crying.

From doing this exercise you may be experiencing a lot of sadness and start crying. You may feel like you can't stop. It is okay, completely okay. Think about how long your body has been storing up this suppressed energy; it is going to come out with some force.

Acceptance is also accepting that they have died and that 'we' cannot control life. When we imagine how our life should be, and it doesn't work out that way, it can literally freak us out. This is what happened to me, and it has happened to most of us. Some parents will never experience what we have gone through, but that is not their fault; the plain truth is that is life. It sounds harsh, but it is true. This is the hand they we have been given and we can either accept it, and feel it, face it, or push it away and let it continue to fester away within us.

Death ends a life; it doesn't end a relationship

Death ends a life; it does not end a relationship. Morrie Schwartz, in his book, *Tuesdays with Morrie*, says, 'As long as we can love each other, and remember the feeling of love we had, you can die, without really ever going away. All the love you created, is still there, all the memories are still there. You live on in the hearts of everyone you have touched, and nurtured while you were here ... Death ends a life, not a relationship.'

Did you feel that? You are doing great. This is big. It is. Now are you ready for another exercise? If not, just come back to it when you feel up to it. With your non-dominant writing hand, I want you to write a letter *from your child to you*. What would he or she say about you as their mum or dad?

If you are righthanded use your left hand, if you are lefthanded use your right hand, and if you are ambidextrous use the hand you least use. John Bradshaw encourages us to do this, as it is though the child within you comes out to say what you need to say.

Turn the page to see what I believe Emma would have said to me.

Why Me?

To my mummy,

I know that you are feeling very, very sad and that you miss me terribly. I miss your smell, cuddles and tenderness.

I am sorry, that I could not stay, my wee heart was tired Mummy, and it wasn't your fault that I got sick and didn't grow properly. I know that part of you has felt guilty for not realising that you had not been fully immunised before you became pregnant, but Mummy that is not your fault. You didn't know. I know that you only wanted the best for me, and you were the best mummy to me.

I know you long to hold me and that you miss my smiles and staring into my blue eyes. I loved melting into your beautiful hazel eyes Mummy. I saw and felt so much love and kindness in your eyes. You are so beautiful to me.

Mummy, you have so much love to give, please do not be overly sad, and please have more babies. The world needs more mummies like you, you would have done anything for me! Anything. I would have loved to meet my new brothers or sisters, but that will have to wait.

Be brave Mummy and keep my memory alive. Please tell my new brothers and sister about me. They need to know that I was part of their family too. And mummy, if our story helps other mummies and daddies to stop feeling so sad and lost, help them Mummy, help them see that they too have lots of love to give just like you. They need help to understand that. You give the best hugs ever.

I would have been 32 years old this year Mummy and probably a mummy myself.

I love you.
I cherish you.
And I will love you forever and ever.

Love from your sweetest daughter Emma Xxx

Now it's your turn.

Can I just give you a big hug? I am so proud of you.

Letting go is helping us heal. We are not letting go of their memory, we are letting go of our anxiety and pain, and our story of how we thought life 'should' have been. Telling our story to ourselves (writing) or sharing it with someone you can trust is so important, because as Dr van der Kolk said *'without stories, the memory becomes frozen, and without memory, you cannot imagine how things would be different.'*

If now was not a good time for you, come back to this when you can, okay?

You've got this.

CHAPTER 12

An Unexpected Gift

> 'The key to a successful life is trust life,
> that is the foundation of everything.
> To "Hope" is to be open to surprise –
> If you trust life, it will surprise you,
> and it will always give you good things.'
> Brother David Steindl-Rast

About a month after the first anniversary of the Emma's death, we were just hanging in there as a couple, we were still struggling with intimacy and expressing our emotions, the rawness of her death was still there, our hearts had been torn apart. We seemed to be having this 'love/hate' relationship, one minute we loved being together and the next minute we couldn't stand each other. The question you both need to ask yourselves as a couple is , 'Do I want this to work?' because it is going to take work and it is not going to be easy. It requires patience, and understanding when you least feel like it. You will feel like giving up. You need to be really honest with each other, it is uncomfortable, but you need to have this conversation. We did. We had to remember why we got together in the first place. For me, Neil was my friend; and for him, he loved me. At the end of the day, we couldn't imagine not having each other in our lives. So, to make this relationship work, we had to put down some boundaries and accept that there were new thoughts and feelings in our marriage that weren't there previously. You are 'allowed' to ask what you want in a relationship.

I had a spiritual urge and Neil didn't. No-one was right no-one was wrong, it was accepting what each other wanted and needed to move forward.

What is a Boundary? A Boundary is a safeguard. Boundaries have a consequence. The purpose is to protect our Joy and Aliveness.

We discussed the idea of having more children and being parents again. It was exciting but terrifying. We knew how fragile life was and wondered how we would cope as a couple if we went through another loss as this was 'OUR' reality. But in the words of Alfred Lord Tennyson, *'Tis better to have loved and lost, than never to have loved at all.* We decided to try for another baby.

As you know, one of the things that can consume you is the desperation of getting pregnant. There is all this focus on that critical time of the month when you are ovulating. Rather than going with the flow and making love, you feel like it is very mechanical, you are just trying to 'get the job done'. This is where we were at, we seemed to be trying but nothing was happening. So, we made an appointment with our doctor. Quite simply he advised us to stop trying so hard and start enjoying each other again, we are supposed to be making love, we are not love machines. We did, and 'Bob's your uncle', it happened: a baby was made.

An Unexpected Gift

Pregnant

I had missed my period. My doctor's nurse took a pregnancy test and at 7 weeks it was confirmed that we were going to be parents again. Woohoo! An appointment was scheduled to see the doctor again for when baby was 12 weeks. However, when I was 11 weeks pregnant, I discovered blood on my undies, after going to the bathroom. My heart literally sank. I started to think the worst. I found myself stuck to the toilet. I don't remember how long I sat there. My legs couldn't or wouldn't work and I found myself shaking and crying. Finally, I pulled myself together, told my boss what I had discovered, she agreed that I should ring my doctor straight away. I managed to get an emergency appointment that day. I rang Neil and told him the news, he tried to sound positive, but I knew what he was also thinking, 'here we go again'.

My GP's room

As I lay on the examining table, my doctor examined my tummy. After asking a few questions and observing that I was looking worried, he decided to send me for an emergency scan. And you guessed it, one of the questions was, 'Are you sure about your dates?' Talk about déjà vu. This nearly put me into a spin. He managed to arrange an appointment for the end of the day. I thanked him, explaining that I just needed to know one way or the other if I was going to lose this baby, or not. 'I understand', he said.

I rang Neil to let him know the outcome so he could meet me at the hospital. We sat in silence, it was that silence, where nothing needed to be said, we were both thinking the same thing. Once I changed into my gown, I was called through to the room by the sonographer. 'Just pop up on the bed, and I will have a look and see what is going on,' she said. I lay there – I started shaking. *Please let everything be okay*, I was telling myself. I made eye contact with Neil. I could see that he was just as worried as I was.

After a few minutes the sonographer announced, 'I have scanned all the vitals and the babies are fine!' There was stunned silence for a second, what did she say? 'I'm sorry, what did you just say I asked?' She beamed at us, repeating, 'The babies are fine! There is nothing to worry about.'

The *babies* are fine? 'Sorry, are you kidding me?' I asked. She looked confused. 'You said *babies*, not baby. Are you having me on?'

'No, we don't have people on about whether they are having twins or not!'

Oh my God. I started to cry. In the meantime, Neil was jumping up and down. 'We are going to have two babies!' he exclaimed. 'Two!' The sonographer was smiling at Neil's reaction then she looked at me with concern. 'Are you okay,' she asked. 'Yes, but how am I supposed to feed two babies!' I exclaimed.

She just smiled and said, 'Oh so the doctor didn't indicate to you that you might be pregnant with twins?' I shook my head. 'No, the only thing he asked was if my dates were right.' She explained that he asked me that question because when he examined me, he thought I was bigger than my expected dates. Relief poured over me.

We were both very excited, but nervous at the same time. I couldn't help but think about the twins that came through the NICU when we were in there with Emma. We were very aware of the potential risks of carrying twins. But I quickly reminded myself that there were also twins that were born perfectly healthy and without complications. If I was to enjoy this pregnancy, I had to think positive. I couldn't worry about the 'what-ifs', because when I did, it just left me feeling exhausted, depressed and weary.

The twins needed me to be the best mum I could be, both physically and mentally.

Emma will never be forgotten. The twins will learn about their big sister, that they didn't get to meet … yet.

CHAPTER 13

Our Family Grows

'What if I fall? Oh, but my darling, what if you fly?'
Erin Hanson

During my follow-up visit with my GP, Dr Peter Borrie, we agreed that due to my history with Emma and now the extra complications of having twins, this would be my last visit with him and Dr Karine Baker, a specialist in Obstetrics and Gynaecology, would now monitor the health of both myself and the twins. I was so fortunate to have her as my specialist. What she didn't know, wasn't worth knowing about.

Once I got over the initial shock of carrying two babies, it was game on. We needed two of this and two of that. It was an incredible feeling but also a very emotional one. Emma would not be here to meet her new siblings.

Every month a scan was scheduled to keep a close eye on the progress of the twins. This appointment was always met with excitement and trepidation. It was a relief to know that Twin One and Twin Two were growing as they should be, according to my due date. The reality of one twin doing better than the other in utero is common. This was always at the back of my mind.

At 24 weeks gestation, we decided to find out what sex the babies were. Twin One was always head down and bottom up and he was identified as a boy. Twin Two however was not so forthcoming in identifying their gender. Every scan this little one was in a different position. They were determined on keeping their identity a secret until the day of arrival.

I don't know how Twin Two was able to move around so much in the confines of my belly, so there was quite a bit of discussion about how these two babies were going to arrive into the world. There was the possibility of both being delivered naturally, or one naturally and one by caesarean section, or both by caesarean section. Having these frank discussions with Dr Baker was very reassuring. I felt I was in the best hands and really any worries I had were put to rest.

My belly was beginning to protrude very quickly, and my skin felt like it was being stretched to the limit. I knew in myself that the reality of making it to full term (40 weeks) was going to be a miracle. I was already mimicking a mother duck, that is, I wasn't walking along I was waddling along. We were informed that the arrival of the twins from 35 weeks on encountered minimal problems, as all the major organs in the baby are developed, and the baby is literally just putting on fat and growing.

Our Family Grows

5 March 1993

Due to the implications and consequences of Emma's death, a national campaign began to bring awareness to those who may have missed out on their second rubella immunisation shot. A newspaper article was published, sharing our story to raise awareness.

Otago Daily Times

Friday, March 5 1993

Mother-to-be tells of rubella danger

By Barbara Fountain

Mrs Wendy King of Concord did not know she had rubella when she became pregnant. She was one of a group of New Zealand woman who missed out on rubella immunisation in the 70s, a slip that had tragic consequences.

Two years ago, Mrs King (28) noticed an itchy rash of spots on her neck and stomach. Co-workers thought she might have the measles, the doctor thought it was a virus. Not long afterwards she found out she was pregnant. Her first baby Emma was born by caesarean section at 31 weeks after failing to thrive in the womb.

Emma had rubella (German measles) and died from complications when she was 19 weeks old.

Now, two years later, Mrs King and her husband Neil are expecting twins.
They have had time to grieve for Emma and Mrs King wants other woman to know about the consequences of contracting rubella during pregnancy.
She said she went through her first pregnancy doing everything right. 'I didn't smoke, and I didn't drink. I had heard about rubella, but I did not know what it did.' She had no idea how she contracted the virus.

Emma was 840gm when she was born.

'To look at her she was perfect.' But the rubella had caused a serious heart condition, cataracts in her eyes, she needed oxygen because she could not breathe properly and had to be tube fed, because she did not have the energy to suck.

The Kings had Emma at home for seven weeks during her short life.
She died just hours before she was to have an operation on her eyes. The rubella immunisation programme changed in the 70s, and it is likely that Mrs King missed out on being immunised when the policy was changed.

Otago Medical School researchers Drs Charlotte Paul and Nigel Dickson found last year that changes to the immunisation policy meant that woman born in the years 1965 to 1967 were much less likely to have been immunised as children than woman born before or after.

> Dr Paul said yesterday, it was possible about a third of woman aged between 25 and 27 were not immunised as children. It was important for all woman, even if they had been immunised, to have their immunity checked before having children, she said. They could not be immunised once they were pregnant.
>
> Mrs King said other people's reactions to her concerns about rubella were strange. 'They treat you like you are a "one-off" case and think it won't happen to anyone else. Even though Emma died, people don't seem to register that it was serious.' She recounts the story of a close friend who became pregnant and had not checked whether she was immune.

9 March 1993

It was 12:30 am on 9 March 1993, when I untangled myself from the sheets to go to the bathroom, again. I was certain the twins thought my bladder was a trampoline, but this time it was different. When I stepped out of bed, I thought I had lost control of my bladder, but no, my waters had broken. The twins were on their way, we had made it to 34-and-a-half week's gestation.

I rang my midwife to advise her that my waters had broken. She instructed me to go back to bed, rest, and then ring her once the contractions were five minutes apart. Then we were to meet her at the hospital. Well, you guessed it, how could one possibly go back to bed, rest or sleep, when my babies were starting their journey into the world?!

At 7:30 am we were on our way to the hospital. On arriving at Queen Mary Hospital, I was meet by a sweet Irish midwife, Mary Gamble. Ginny, my chosen midwife, had been up through the night with a complicated birth and would join us soon. At 2.00 pm, seven hours had passed, and progress had slowed. My contractions were so intense and painful, that I announced to my two midwives, that if I did not get an epidural soon, I would find a knife and get these babies out myself! (Just remember all pregnancies and births are different.) I soon got my wish. The natural way in my experience was overrated, the world was a better place once my epidural had kicked in. In Matthew Perry's words 'Could the pain, be any more intense!'

At 7:00 pm I was told to start pushing. Twin One was head down and was always going to be the first one out. I pushed and pushed, but Twin One was not in any hurry. A decision was made by the doctors to help Twin One move a little bit quicker as Twin Two's heart rate was going through the roof. Twin One, Blair, was born with forceps at 7:32 pm. He weighed 4 pound 15 ounces.

Twin Two, Regan, after having to share his space in the womb with his older brother decided to flip around, as he now had the whole womb to himself. Ah, the bed to myself, at last he must have been thinking! His heart rate was now normal however, he was now lying in a transverse position and had to be pulled out feet first into the world. Regan was born at 7:38 pm weighing 4 pound 11 ounces with a cleft-lip and palate.

Both twins needed assistance to breathe, but they were soon responding on their own. It wasn't long before I had two dear little boys wrapped up tightly in warm towels placed in my arms. The tears rolled down my face. I felt like the luckiest mother in the world!

Our Family Grows

Twin Two – Regan's cleft-lip and palate

Regan's cleft lip and palate were never picked up in the scans. This was due to the technology available at the time. So for him to present this congenital birth defect on his arrival was a bit of a surprise to Dr Baker (my specialist), Dr Barrie Taylor (our paediatric specialist), Ginny and Mary (the midwifes), and both myself and Neil.

Advancements in technology means that scans can now show pretty much every little detail, whilst the baby is growing in utero. Any concerns are picked up earlier, so parents and physicians are prepared. With saying that, Regan's conditions did not concern me one iota. All I wanted to know was how was I going to feed this darling baby. I was elated that he did not have a life-threatening condition and that he had arrived safely. We were soon to learn that modern medicine was going to right this birth defect. This was no mean feat though. Regan was a courageous strong young man that had to go through 21 surgeries.

> Note: What did Regan's care look like for the next 20 years? Between dental surgeries and plastic surgeries, (a total of 21 surgeries in all) meant Regan's life for the next 20 years involved many trips to Dunedin Public Hospital and the Dental School. From day two of Regan being born he was under the care of the Dental School. Eithne McFadyen looked after Regan for the first few years of Regan's dental care then his care was taken over by Associate Professor Kumara De Silva in his teens. However, from 4 months of age to 21 years of age Regan's surgeon and Otolaryngologist Dr Jeff Robinson was an integral part of Regan's journey under the Dunedin Public Hospital and Mercy Hospital

> and Dr Jeff will always have a special place in our hearts. We were so grateful we lived in a city that had the Dental School and wonderful doctors, because other parents in the surrounding Otago Area had to factor in day trips or overnight stays with their little one for their appointments.

Mixed emotions

It had been a massive day. I was exhausted but elated at the same time. Blair and Regan were taken up to the NICU to be monitored as they had arrived five and half weeks early. All their vital signs would be thoroughly checked out, which also meant they would be in their own incubator until they could both regulate their own body temperature.

All I wanted to do was sleep. I had been awake since 12:30 am that morning and I was emotionally relieved and physically shattered. I will see my babies again tomorrow and find out what the plan is with Regan. One day at a time, I kept telling myself, one day at a time.

The following day

I awoke with excitement and anticipation of seeing my babies, even though I had tossed and turned with the battle damage incurred in the nether regions, this was insignificant to the little bundles of joy that were waiting upstairs in NICU.

As soon as I was able, the orderly wheeled me up to the 5th floor to hold my babies. Whilst the nurses were attending to the other babies, I just sat there and took in the sight of my wee boys until the nurses was free to place them in my arms. My heart swelled with joy when the nurses attending to Regan and Blair related to me what happened when Regan became unsettled in the night. They took Blair out of his incubator and placed him beside Regan. What happened you ask? Regan stopped crying and calmed down immediately. His big brother could give him the comfort he needed even though I couldn't be there. This was just another magical moment of the bond twins can have with each other.

When you think about it, it isn't that surprising – they had shared their home together in the womb for 34-and-a-half weeks. It must have felt strange for them being in a new environment and not getting a foot or an arm shoved into each other.

During the night Blair graduated from the incubator to a cot. I held Blair first and automatically introduced him to my breast to see if he would suckle. He did. It never ceases to amaze me how their instinct is to search out the smell of their mother and move their little mouth for nutrition and comfort.

After attending to Blair, I moved over towards Regan. Regan was still in his incubator, he had vomited a few times in the night, and had a tube inserted via his nose into his tummy so he could receive fluids. This is when the flood of emotions unexpectedly hit me. Nothing prepared me for this. I went from having a beautiful bonding session with Blair and now I am sobbing uncontrollably.

There I was staring at Regan in his incubator, but I couldn't see Regan. I could only see Emma. My mind associated the incubator with Emma. The more I tried to stop the river of tears, the worse I became. I felt the gentle hand of the head nurse, Thea Leveak on my back. I said to her through the tears, 'we have to stop meeting

Why Me?

like this.' You see Thea had also been the head nurse in NICU when Emma was there. 'It will be okay Wendy,' she said. 'It will be okay. Regan will soon look like his brother. The plastic surgeon and dental surgeon will be over today to talk about the procedures to rectify this.' I turned and looked at her. Her eyes were glassy, and her face was soft and kind. Little did she know, that this was not the reason for my tears.

I tried to stop sobbing to get the words out. 'Thea,' I said, 'I am not worried about Regan's cleft lip and palate. All I can see when I look in the incubator is Emma. All I see is Emma. Emma should be here. I love Regan, but I miss my girl. I just want to hold her. I just want her.' I sobbed. 'Oh Wendy,' she said, and tears began to stream down her face too.

Talk about an emotional roller-coaster ride. I had leapt from anticipation and joy, to great sadness. Today I was missing my Emma and feeling guilty for momentarily feeling so happy. It was so exhausting to wrestle with being sad and happy at the same time. I didn't know at the time, but these feelings and emotions were completely normal. My brain's last experience and memory catalogued the sight of a baby in an incubator as Emma, that is why I felt sad because it wasn't her.

Over the next few days, it was trial and error getting Regan's feeding routine sorted, and his ability to suck from a bottle. It wasn't a regular bottle, it was a Haberman bottle with a valve in between the teat and bottle. As he couldn't suck, I would squeeze a small amount of milk into his mouth, and he would swallow. Feeding Regan would take up to an hour and half, because when you were squeezing the milk into his mouth you were also squeezing air into his mouth. If you didn't stop to wind him, air would build up inside his tummy which then caused him to projectile vomit. I have to tell you, when you did stop to wind Regan, boy could he burp! Very impressive indeed!

The days were passing very quickly in the hospital; a week had flown by. The boys were situated on the fifth floor of the hospital and the maternity ward was on the second floor. This meant many trips backward and forwards in the lift for feeding times and cuddles. As Blair was thriving it was suggested that I take Blair home, and travel in each day to see Regan. That suggestion was a definite no! I was not leaving the hospital without my two babies, they arrived together they were going to go home together. Seeing the bond, the twins had between them and then separating them would not be in the best interests of Regan or my psyche.

It was three weeks before we all went home together.

CHAPTER 14

Letting Go of the Fear

*'God, grant me the serenity to accept the things I
cannot change,
the courage to change the things I can,
and the wisdom to know the difference.'*
Reinhold Niebuhr

Sometimes I wonder how I managed to survive physically and mentally when we left the hospital and went home with Blair and Regan. Neil had recently started a new job which meant he was only home with me and the boys for two days. Yep, that was the total of our parental leave requirement together and it was all hands to the pump for me. Literally! As Regan could not suckle or attach himself to the breast, I didn't want him to miss out on my breast milk, so I hired an electric breast pump to express my milk, and then I would transfer my milk into his bottle. I managed to express my milk for 6 weeks. However, expressing milk, then feeding Regan then breastfeeding Blair was becoming unmanageable. How so?

Why Me?

For the first four months of our busy family life, it would take me approximately 10–20 minutes to feed Blair and 60–90 minutes to feed Regan. I juggled this feeding routine by feeding Blair first from one breast, whilst jiggling Regan in the bouncinette with my foot, then swap them over. Then I would give Regan a quarter of his bottle, wind and burp him, then put him back in the bouncinette, then finish feeding Blair on the other breast, put him in the bouncinette, then take as long as it took with Regan. It was quite a system that I created, but it worked. Doing it this way meant I had no babies crying to be feed.

To assist Regan with feeding, Regan was fitted with a plastic mouth plate that covered the roof of his mouth. This required a fortnightly trip into the Dunedin Dental School to have a mold taken of his mouth to make the plate. Then another trip back in the next day or two to collect it. There were only two occasions, where the mold impression wasn't precise enough, which resulted in a loose plate. This meant it had to be redone, which required another trip back into the Dental School. The needed to happen every two weeks, due to Regan growing, and his mouth changing. If this wasn't done, it would be a bit like having a pair of false teeth without the teeth, rattling around in your mouth. Once Regan was six months old, he would have his first surgery which involved closing his lip, which meant he would no longer require a plate to feed. It was a matter of digging deep and doing what needed to be done!

It was a busy, busy time. Would I do it all over again? In a heartbeat. But the lack of sleep and exhaustion did take its toll.

Scared of losing one or both twins

One of the biggest fears after losing a child, is the thought of it happening again. You know how fragile life is. In the blink of an eye, your entire world, your whole reason for living can be ripped away from you. That is how I felt at the time, I just wanted to be a mum. I tried not to focus on my fear, but it was always there hovering at the back of my mind.

To be honest, for the first 10 months of Blair and Regan's life I put a mental wall up to protect myself. I wanted to be engaged and close as a mum but not too close, if that makes any sense. I attended to the needs of my babies, I sang to them, I told them about their big sister, I took them for walks in the pram, but I couldn't emotionally attach myself to them. Unconsciously I was letting fear run my life. I thought that the minute I absolutely absorb, every bit of these boys, something tragic would happen. I felt so blessed to have them both and yet I felt that it was too good to be true. I know now that this is a normal reaction to my experience with Emma because trauma is the lasting effects of emotional shock. You are not only dealing with the 'effects' of trauma but you are also dealing with past experiences that affect your thinking, and self-worth. It's knowing the difference between you 'deserve to be happy' and that you are 'worthy' of happiness.

One of my worries with the twins, is that Blair would always sleep longer than Regan, and if Blair hadn't woken up within half an hour of Regan, I would always think the worst. I would brace myself as I walked into their bedroom, always expecting to find Blair dead. I had to find a way for this to stop as it was ruining me physically and emotionally. Adding to my catastrophising was a memory of an English assignment that was given to our class when I was 11 years of age. The teacher gave us a scenario that if we were in the car with our parents and two other siblings and we crashed into a ravine, and we only had the chance to save one member, who would it be and why? I know what you are thinking. What?

This scenario troubled me greatly, given the fact that regular trips were required by myself with two helpless babies, to and from either the dental school, or Dunedin Public Hospital. I was a very cautious driver and if anyone appeared to be in a hurry, I gave them a wide berth. I knew that if I were to be in a car accident, I may only be able to help one of my babies. These gorgeous babies were here with me now, and the thought of losing one ... I felt that would be the end of me. So, my way of dealing with my fear at the time, was to disconnect emotionally from them. This was my way of coping back then. I just didn't think I could survive the loss of another child.

A new perspective

I thought that by disconnecting myself emotionally from the boys I was protecting myself from further hurt and that it was a clever tactic. What I failed to realise was that while I was disconnected from my emotions, I was also missing out on the joy of each milestone that I should have been celebrating.

I cannot remember precisely what day it was, but I caught myself laughing while the two of them were interacting with each other in their Jolly Jumpers. They LOVED being in their Jolly Jumpers. They used to get upset if I unstrapped the harness from the spring before they were finished jumping or twirling around. I would set the Jolly Jumpers up so that they were facing each other in the doorways and could watch each other bouncing up and down. This would set them into fits of giggles and laughter.

While they were giggling, they were also doing these little moves with their feet as if they were puppets performing in the Irish *Riverdance*, and the more they laughed at each other the more they pointed their toes. They used their feet to push off the ground to spin, wriggle and bounce. It was just hilarious! They were laughing, and I was laughing. Their eyes were sparkling, they were so happy. They were laughing at me laughing, I started laughing harder, to the point where there were tears of laughter running down my face. I felt so happy. I had a warmth running through my body. I caught myself off guard. My boys were talking gibberish to each other. I had stopped laughing, so they were trying to make me laugh again.

It just occurred to me that I had just experienced the biggest aha moment. I knew from this day forward that I could not shut down my emotions any longer.

I realised I had two choices. I could continue to remain emotionally distant to protect myself or allow myself to become vulnerable, and enjoy these two little humans every moment of every day. I was worrying about something that may never happen, and I couldn't control it anyway. I had to let go of the fear. What I also didn't realise was how much energy it was taking from me to be in this mind state.

It was scary to let go, but Dr Bessel van der Kolk in his book, *The Body Keeps the Score*, says it all regarding this matter:

> '*If we are stuck in survival mode, its energies are focused on fighting off unseen enemies, which leaves no room for nurture, care and love. As long as the mind is defending itself against invisible assaults, our closest bonds are threatened along with our ability to imagine, plan, play, learn and pay attention to other people's needs.*'

We must accept that we cannot control life. We can plan, but unforeseen circumstances can and will happen to anyone at any time! The trouble is, until you have been touched by the effects of death, you take life for granted and as my teacher said right at the beginning of this book, we never know what is around the corner. The issue is how many of us are taught the 'HOW' of life skills if we were to encounter such an event.

The boys were a lot of work but were such fun. People would make the comment, when they saw us together, 'oh no, double trouble' and I would say, 'oh yes, double cuddles.' We were content as a family of four until the boys started school. We decided to try for another baby. We were blessed with two more children, Mitchell Scott King born on 29 December 1998 and Charlotte Rose King born 18 September 2000.

However, little did we know that we would be hit with another curve ball in February 2002.

CHAPTER 15

Thrown a Curve Ball

'The greatest glory in living lies not in never falling, but in rising, every time we fall.'
Nelson Mandela

It was the morning of 28 February 2002 and the twins were nearly nine, Mitch was three and Charlotte was 18 months old. Emma would have just had her eleventh birthday.

Our home was always like a busy train station on a school day. Once the twins went off to school, I would set Mitchell and Charlotte up in the lounge with a *Thomas the Tank Engine* or *High Five* video, whilst I briefly scanned the morning *Otago Daily Times* and had my third or fourth cup of half-cold tea. For some reason, I could never finish one, and I was forever finding half-drunk cups of tea in the lounge or bedroom.

That morning, when I unfolded the paper the bold headline on the front page stopped me in my tracks. Usually, I would turn to the back of the page first to read 'matched, hatched and dispatched' that is, (births, deaths and marriages) The headline on the front page stopped me in my tracks; it read:

> *'Hospitals legally entitled to keep hearts,' says expert*
> *Greenlane Hospital, New Zealand's Premier heart facility yesterday revealed it had kept about 1350 hearts from babies and children in a 'heart library'. The collection began in 1950. Most of the hearts had been taken from the bodies of children who died of congenital heart disease. There were also a few adult hearts.*
> *At the time, parental or caregiver consent to retain hearts, was not seen as an issue, partly because most of the hearts were removed for post-mortems, and it was within the coroner's jurisdiction for the heart to be retained for detailed examination by a pathologist.*

At that point I couldn't read on. I thought I was going to be sick, my ears started ringing and I thought I was also going to pass out. Oh no, no, no, don't tell me they could possibly have Emma's heart.

I slowly stood up. I wanted to scream but I couldn't. I sat down again because I felt faint. I tried to keep reading, but my eyes could not focus. I needed to calm down and take some breaths. My legs felt like jelly. Mitchell and Charlotte were completely oblivious as to what was happening to me and I was scared that I would pass out and then for them to find their mummy passed out on the floor, it would scare the living daylights out of them.

I started taking in deep breaths. Once I felt like I was in control, I walked outside. I needed air. Oh, my goodness, my thoughts were going a hundred miles an hour. *Don't tell me after all this time, they have Emma's heart.* I told myself to calm down. Surely, they would have asked me if they wanted to take her heart for further investigation. It took me at least another hour until I could get a grip of myself to continue reading the article. It continued (abbreviated):

> Greenlane reviewed its heart library last year after an inquiry in Britain due to a scandal involving a hospital that retained thousands of body parts without consent.
> The hospital last year formed a steering group, which includes parent representatives and iwi, to ensure the collection was managed appropriately, and hearts were not being kept against relatives wishes.
> Greenlane had admitted taking the hearts of over 1000 babies or children without consent for research purposes.
> Dr Finucane said since the late 1980s there had been a greater awareness of consent issues. While a process for seeking consent had not been formalised, she was sure in most cases consent to keep body parts would have been sought.
> She said that the steering group knew that 'it was wrong' to take the hearts without consent. 'We all regret the grief that we have caused people who are going to find this out and be very upset by it,' she told National Radio.
> 'But it was the practice of the day when a post-mortem was done to remove the organs at times and to get a detailed examination. Without that we couldn't get the correct feedback to the family as to what the cause of death was.'
> Health Minister Annette King said today that it was too early to say if an official inquiry was needed into the organ controversy. She said that before 1996, there was no proper legal consents for hospitals to follow. She wanted to make sure that consent to take organs was sought by authorities after 1996.
> Greenlane's library was credited with enabling New Zealand surgeons to make major advances in heart surgery, saving the lives of many children with heart disease. As far fewer

children or babies now died from heart complications only a few hearts were collected, with parental permission each year. Dr Finucane said the hearts were well documented and it would not be difficult to confirm whose hearts had been kept right back until 1950.

Green Party health spokeswoman Sue Kedgley said there should be a ministerial inquiry into how the babies' hearts were removed without their parents' consent and stored in the library.

'There are incredibly serious ethical and informed consent issues that need to be addressed if we are to avoid a repetition of this bizarre and tragic episode,' Ms Kedgley said in a statement. It was 'almost unbelievable' that after the Cartwright inquiry a hospital had knowingly extracted hearts from babies and stored them for research without first getting permission from the parents.

I just sat in silence, stunned. There was a very high chance that they could have Emma's heart as she was a 'one off' case. At the bottom of the article was a hotline number to call if you thought there was a possibility the hospital could be holding your child's heart.

After reading the article, I wondered around in a daze and caught myself shaking and crying. I attempted to ring Neil, but each time I picked the phone up, I couldn't get any words out. It was like reliving Emma's death all over again.

You may be justified in thinking that even though these actions were unethical, it did help save babies lives. But that wasn't the point. It was that it was underhanded, deceitful and it was done in secret. They had stolen parts of our precious babies. I am all for research for medical advancement, don't get me wrong, there was a strong possibility that if we were asked if they could have Emma's heart for medical research, we would have granted it. However, right at this moment it was hard to get my head around this news.

I waited until Neil arrived home that evening. I still couldn't speak. I heard gravel crunching under the tyres of the car and went to meet Neil at the door. I handed him the paper. His eyes meet my eyes. He could tell by looking at my facial expression and red eyes that something had rocked my world. He was just as dumbfounded as I was.

I had three attempts ringing the hotline number and each time I had to hang up as I couldn't get the words out; *'do you have my daughter's heart?'* It was a story that shocked the nation. Many parents were not aware hearts, or other organs were retained after autopsies of their children or aborted foetuses. Almost 3000 people had called the hotline, and just under 40 people had been told that their child's organs had been retained. The following news articles that appeared in the *Dunedin Otago Daily Times* make interesting reading.

Otago Daily Times

Friday, 1 March 2002

Thirty-four years after her baby son died at Greenlane Hospital, long serving *Otago Daily Times* Alexandra reporter DIANNE KING is waiting to hear if the hospital has kept his heart. She prays it did not.

My heart aches.

Not just for our family but for every other parent who is waiting to hear whether their baby's heart has been stored without their knowledge at the Greenlane Hospital, Auckland.

As parents, Bryan and I are in a state of limbo – just like the one we experienced 34 years ago – waiting to hear back from Greenlane about our baby's heart.

Yesterday morning I rang the 0800. There was still a queue but about 10.30am I made contact at least.

The cardiac-paediatric liaison nurse, Heather, was warm and caring as she took the details, explaining the news broke earlier than expected although the hospital knew a documentary was being made.

But we wait again, because it will be Monday before we know whether we buried all our baby son in Roxburgh Cemetery, days into the New Year in 1968.

Today, for thousands of parents like us, old wounds are open, hearts ache and tears flow as memories flood and I've that "empty arms" feeling only parents who lose a child will probably understand.

Why was I standing in the shower crying yesterday morning?

On December 4, 1967, Matthew David Waigth King was born in Roxburgh Hospital where his brothers had arrived in earlier years.

I never got to hold this newborn babe in my arms. He was whisked away to Dunedin Hospital within an hour of his birth and, days later, he was flown to Greenlane Hospital, Auckland.

For three weeks we waited. Two days after Christmas, our wonderful parents paid the airfares and took our two children and we flew to Auckland to be there for our tiny son, managing to sneak our cuddles the night before his operation.

I don't need to shut my eyes to see surgeon Mr Brian Barratt-Boyes and a colleague gently saying our baby had only a 40%–60% chance of surviving the operation.

Hours later we are back, because Matthew did not survive, but these two men were wonderful, explaining that when they opened him up, his tiny little heart was worse than they thought – it was in reverse order.

As we heard news of the heart bank on television on Wednesday night, Bryan said: "Would they keep it because they told us his was so bad?"

As a mother I've a dilemma; as a father so has Bryan, because as parents, if his heart is still at Greenlane, what decision will we make on Monday?

Please God, were we among the lucky ones? Because we're trying not to think about burying his heart 34 years later and we're sad the hospital, which had shown compassion to two young parents from Central Otago, has found itself in this position.

We were distressed parents when his operation failed, the only consolation being the surgeons' assurances every operation helped another child, which was and has been for 34 years a comfort to us.

So we wait again, grateful for the three healthy children we've had since, plus six little "grandies", including Benjamin Matthew King, who takes the name after another generation. But my heart aches still.

Otago Daily Times

Friday, March 1 2002

Worried Parents Flood Switchboard

By Joanna Norris and NZPA

Otago parents were among hundreds of people who flooded Greenlane Hospital switchboard with calls yesterday fearing body parts from their children had been retained by the Auckland hospital.

The hospital, home to the country's top cardiac facilities, this week admitted it had a "library" of more than 1300 hearts collected from patients, mainly children with congenital heart diseases dating back to the 1950s.

Greenlane paediatric cardiologist Dr Nigel Wilson told the Otago Daily Times that until the 1990s it was likely the hearts were retained without consent.

"But from 1992 for anyone who died at Greenlane, we had a consent process in place and the intent was to get it, but it's still possible there have been cases where there has not been consent" he said.

Dr Wilson said the hospital was advising people it would probably be up to a week before it could confirm whether their child's heart was at the hospital. "In terms of privacy we have to have a way of knowing the person [making an inquiry] is a relative of the person who died., then we have to check against the records to see if the heart is there. If the answer is no, it's pretty straightforward, but if it is yes, we have to double check."

It emerged yesterday that hundreds of abnormal hearts stored at the hospital were taken from aborted foetuses. At first, Greenlane said the hearts were mainly from children and babies.

But yesterday, the hospital's clinical director of children's heart surgery, Dr Kirsten Finucane, said many were from aborted foetuses. Because of legal worries the hospital would not seek to contact the women involved, who may have had secret abortions.

The hospital had received more than 500 calls from relatives of people concerned the hospital had body parts from their dead children.

One Dunedin woman, who did not want to be named, said she waited on hold for more than four hours and was unable to get through. The news has prompted the Ministry of Health to advise hospitals that any body parts held should be released to families if possible.

Ministry deputy director-general of clinical services Dr Coin Feek said some hospitals and medical schools kept body parts for teaching or research purposes.

"The organisation responsible for these collections should review them from time to time to see if they are still required. If body parts are no longer required, they should be made available to relatives who are able to bury or cremate them", he said in a statement.

Otago medical school Pathology head Dr Colin Geary said for the past 15 years no body parts had been taken from patients without consent, but before 1988, when consent was given for an autopsy, it allowed medical practitioners to take parts to confirm diagnoses, to use in teaching students, for therapeutic purposes such as the extraction of growth hormones and for research.

"Then the Human Tissues Act changed entirely and the permission of the next of kin had to be sought, but even under the old regime the tissues were returned to the body" he said.

He said the medical school had a small museum with specimens dating back 100 years. However, he said it was appropriate the school retained the material for teaching. Otago District Health Board chief executive Bill Adam said Dunedin Hospital did not retain body parts without specific consent.

However, if anyone had concerns about the issue in relation to Dunedin Hospital, they should contact the hospital's patient affairs department on 03 474 0999.

People with concerns in relation to Greenlane Hospital should call 0800 746-445.

Why Me?

Otago Daily Times

Friday, March 1 2002

MATTERS OF THE HEART

REVELATIONS that children's hearts have been kept at Greenlane hospital; for research purposes without the consent of parents is immensely upsetting to many families. Taking body parts or conducting clinical research without families' consent is not acceptable today. That has been made plain for a decade or more by changing societal attitudes and official findings, not least among those of the Cartwright inquiry.

To its credit, Greenlane is doing all it can now to reassure the families concerned and is making arrangements to have the body parts returned if that is the families' wish. Senior Greenlane clinicians are also at pains to point out that such practices are no longer carried out at the hospital. And Health Minister Annette King has moved promptly to reassure the public that they are not carried out elsewhere in New Zealand. Similar reassurances should be forthcoming from the countries medical bodies, particularly for parents and grandparents throughout the country who will be incredulous that such practices could have happened here at all.

But while we can understand the high emotions and reopening of old wounds that the Greenlane disclosures bring, the context in which this "scandal" has occurred must be remembered. Greenlane's "heart library" consists of some 1350 hearts, mainly those of children with congenital deformities, collected since 1950 and preserved for research purposes at the country's top hospital. Following a similar scandal in Britain, the Greenlane hospital began a review last year of its library's contents.

The hospital formed a heart steering group, which includes parent representatives and iwi, to check that the collection was being managed appropriately and that the hearts were not being kept against relatives' wishes. They found some families had no idea they had not buried all of their babies.

It should be remembered that awareness of parents' rights and consent issues now is vastly different to what is was 50, or even 30, years ago. The babies' hearts at Greenlane, and other human tissue, were collected then for research purposes in a paternalistic atmosphere. Patients and their families were passive and trusting recipients of care. Most knew little of the concept of consent, let alone consent procedures, and they rarely questioned medical decisions.

That babies' hearts were taken and kept without parents' knowledge does not mean that all doctors 50 years ago were perverse. That was normal procedure then. Simply, the world has changed, that partly as a result of some shocking cases of medical abuse here and overseas.

Strict ethical guidelines and reviews are in place. No medical research can be contemplated without the consent of the donor or their next of kin and unless subject to proper ethical review. That is the way it should be, judged by today's standards and morals.

Perhaps the most disturbing aspect of the Greenlane disclosure however, is that it appears babies' hearts were being taken without consent, or at least using faulty consent procedures, as late as 1996, well after the Cartwright inquiry had established the principle that no research should be carried out without proper informed consent.

Some clarification and reform of our laws may be needed, particularly aspects of the Human Tissue Act of 1964. But patients and families are protected by more recent legislation, including the code of rights in the Health and Disability Commission Act, where emphasis on consent is prominent. Generally, contemporary medical training is also inculcating these values so that there is clearly a commitment to ethical review among the medical profession.

The distress and grief that the Greenlane revelations cause will vary from family to family. The nation's indignation at such practices is fully justified.

For a public perhaps already skeptical about research in general, it is imperative that practitioners everywhere move swiftly to reassure the public that a new set of values is in place and that medical research is no longer conducted without consent.

Otago Daily Times

Friday, March 1 2002

No samples since 1980s without consent

By Joanna Norris and NZPA

Modern ethical practice should have prevented the retention of babies' hearts at Greenlane Hospital, says Otago University bio-ethics head Prof Donald Evans.

Prof Evans, a member of the National Ethics Committee, said there were clear ethical guidelines which should have prevented samples being collected without consent after the 1980s. His comments come after news that about 1300 hearts have been stored at Greenlane Hospital.

"In the past, the paternalistic approach of hospitals was accepted as the norm, but things have changed hugely in the last 20 to 30 years and we are no longer living in a time when patients are seen as research fodder."

He said revelations in the 1980s that women were the subjects of a cervical cancer study at National Women's Hospital had helped shape ethical policy and the Cartwright Inquiry in 1988 set guidelines for informed consent. The guidelines were clear that no research should be done on humans without consent.

> "What has happened since 1990 is particularly disturbing. What happened before was not right, but one can understand what was going on, but it is hard to understand [post Cartwright] that any patient was used in this way, without consent."
>
> New Zealand Medical Association Chairman Dr John Adams, of Dunedin, said while the retained hearts had helped advance medical research, it was "disturbing" to hear some had been taken without consent.
>
> Otago University medical lawyer Prof Peter Skegg, who has provided advice to Greenlane Hospital, said the hearts may have been collected legally.
>
> He said the Health Tissue Act makes provision for the prevention of organs for science and according to the law, the Act did not require the consent of relatives.

I finally found the courage to pick up the phone and ring the hotline number and snuffled my way through the questions that were asked by a lovely person at the end of the phone.

It was now a waiting game. For me I wasn't handling it very well at all, I just went into this depressive state. It was as if a big black cloud was hovering over me, and I couldn't shake it. It took all my might and energy to function and carry on looking after my wee family.

The waiting was excruciating. I found myself in a constant fog, in a state of anxiety. I was grateful for a friend who saw the situation that I was in and knew that this was not something I could deal with on my own or shake myself out of it. I needed medical help. I rang the doctors' rooms and made an hour appointment to discuss my situation with my GP.

My visit with Dr Astrid Windfuhr

Dr Astrid had been my new GP since the twins were approximately 18 months old. She was always attentive, kind and understanding. She never knew about our first baby Emma as there never seemed to be occasion for it to be discussed at previous doctors' appointments with either myself or the children. I told her my story about our beautiful Emma and how the news in the paper about the 'heart library' had set me into a spin. The waiting to know if they had taken her heart for research purposes was doing my head in.

After listening to my story and seeing the state I was in, she gave me some medication to deal with anxiety and depression and said that she would make inquiries on my behalf as to what happened at Emma's autopsy and ask for a copy of the report. On obtaining the report, she would ring me and go through it with me.

I can't remember how long it took to find out the results, but I do remember my GP ringing me to say that she had the report and that Emma's heart had not been taken for medical research. I burst into tears. I was so relieved. She invited me to make an hour appointment with her, and she would go through the report with me. I was so grateful to have a kind and caring doctor through a very difficult time.

CHAPTER 16

I'm here with you and for you!

> 'Turn your wounds into wisdom.'
> Oprah Winfrey

How are you doing? It's tough, isn't it? You know as I do – 'EVERY MOMENT, EVERY MINUTE MATTERS, but it is what you do next that matters the most!'

You may have been living with the loss of your loved one for a very long time or maybe you are trying to make sense of your new reality. It can be so overwhelming. You may feel as if the 'wheels have really fallen off in your life', metaphorically that is. Wherever you are, I want to help you either get the wheels back on, or stop you from hobbling along with flat tyres. But for change to happen we have to do something we have never done before.

Remember the parable at the beginning of the book about the man who suffers from his disease in the hole? Some people appreciate the situation you are in, but they don't know the way out. I do. I have spent thousands of dollars researching, and understanding what makes us tick and what happens to our mind and body in traumatic events. Why?

Because we were only educated on how to accomplish and acquire status or possessions, not on 'how to be'. As Oscar Wilde said:

> 'To live is the rarest thing in the world;
> most people exist, and that is all.'

There is so much to learn about ourselves. Why we think the way we do, and why we do the things that we do.

It is about bringing awareness to where you are right now. Being honest with yourself about what you are going to do with the rest of your life. It is about healing and coming out of the 'trance' of suffering.

My goal is not only to help you to reduce life's pain but in the words of John Bradshaw, an American educator, author and counsellor who has now passed, described in his book, *Homecoming*: *'The goal is to is to become a balanced, empowered creative human being, who doesn't have to hide behind my recovery, and I don't have to talk about how screwed up, I am anymore.'*

I would like you to think of me as a friend who is also a teacher, coach and trainer. Trainer because there are some new disciplines, we need to learn to retrain our mind. Like anything new, it requires practice and patience. Remember, *'you only know what you know'*. If we want to understand ourselves, we need to understand our history, because the emotional scars of our past will follow us.

I realised that I had less summers ahead of me than behind me, and I wanted my days to count. I wanted to feel free and alive!

I'm here with you and for you!

The lessons In Part 2 of this book will change your perspective of life.

If you are willing to explore, have an open mind and heart you will learn something new. I even had my own Aha moment when I was writing this book, in the editing process.

My publisher Natasha Denman told me this would happen to me. She was right. I had an epiphany, a moment of sudden realisation that I would love to share with you about the loss of my Emma, it was …

'I am living for you, not dying because of you.'
Wendy B King

A new mantra 'I am living for you, not dying because of you!' I am, I am living for you!

Are you ready to know the secret of how to get out of the hole? Today is a new day, a new chapter in your 'book of life'. Are you ready to turn the page with me?

Part 2

12 Lessons for Healing that you Didn't Know you Needed to Hear

*'We cannot solve our problems
with the same thinking that created them.'*
Albert Einstein

You only know what you know.

If only I could break free...

wbk
WENDY B KING

LESSON 1

Our EGO

I have a thought – I am not my thoughts

> 'You become what you believe.'
> Oprah Winfrey

I would like you to reflect on the image of the little elephant and the big elephant.

What do you see?

Do you see the situation as hopeless as the big elephant does? Or do you see what I see? You know as I do, that the adult elephant could easily break free from the little chain and peg. I can hear you saying, 'Just try, just be curious. If you just lift your leg, or move it slightly you would be free'. Free from what he believed, and thought as a young elephant.

His memory as a little elephant was, that it didn't matter how many times he tugged at the peg and chain, he could not break free. That was his conditioning, that was 'his thoughts'. He did not realise that as he became bigger and stronger that he would one day have the strength to break free. The little elephant was conditioned to what 'he knew'. Is that you? Do you tell yourself that you are stupid, not good enough, or unlovable, or deserve to be treated badly?

We are sometimes like the adult elephant – we only know what we know. It's our thoughts, beliefs or experiences that have convinced us that they are true, without questioning or challenging them. You may have been told by a parent, caregiver or teacher that 'you are stupid' when you were a child. Comments like that can really hurt and leave an emotional scar on us for the rest of our life, because we may believe it is true. But is it true? It is an opinion – it is not true. This is how we can get caught up in unhelpful self-talk. It's the unconscious bias you have towards an area of your life that you accept without questioning or believing there are other possibilities or ways. It is so important that we are aware of this.

The relationship we have between our ego (our thought process – our conditioning) and our body is everything.

Our thoughts can have a major impact on our ability to feel and heal from this traumatic event. Our thoughts can get us into a lot of trouble.

We can get so caught up in our thoughts and believe they are true. Remember early on in my story, when I was being punished as a child? I thought that I must be a very bad person for God to allow such punishments. That was my thought, that was my belief. But was it true? No. Thoughts are not facts.

It can be difficult to separate this, but we must. We must be able to know the difference between 'I have a thought' and 'I am not my thought'. The difference between 'I made a mistake' and 'I am a mistake', 'I failed that test' and 'I am a failure'. We must notice the difference in the language we use. We need to recognise that you are in charge of your mind and not the other way around. Our thoughts, 'our ego', can cause much disruption and unnecessary pain in our life.

I want you to think of your ego as a back seat driver in your car. Have you ever experienced someone, giving you unsolicited advice when you are driving? They are trying to tell you how to drive, where to drive and how fast to go? It is annoying and unhelpful isn't it. So next time you hear that chitter chatter of voices going on in your head, tell it to be quiet, or ask yourself:

- By **'listening'** to these thoughts what purpose is it serving me?
- Be **'aware'** of what is happening.
- **'Notice'** how often it has something to say.
- **'Tell it'**, your ego, (mind and thoughts), 'thank you for your help, but I do not need it; be gone!'

YOU are in the driver's seat and just like your mind, you get to decide what you feed it. Have the courage to break free from your old thought patterns.

Just like the illustration, you know that the adult elephant could easily break free from his situation. The question is do you believe you can do the same? Just like Oprah said, 'You become what you believe'.

Keep a look out for my *'Attitude and Gratitude'* journal which will soon be available.

Friendship is not about who you've known the longest. It's about who walked into your life, said "I'm here for you" and proved it.

LESSON 2

Our Precious Friends

'A friend in need is a friend indeed.'
Benjamin Franklin

We need you!

I know it is not easy for you, because we naturally sense each other's distress, and who wants to feel that? The irony is that you can't speed grief up; contrary to what you have been told, it is not a process; it is a journey. You learn to adapt and adjust, to your new pathway or chapter of life. Everyone adapts to it differently.

If you saw a little girl or little boy crouched down hugging their legs and sobbing, would you walk past them, or would you bend down and ask kindly, 'Honey what happened, are you okay?'

Honestly, that is how we feel when our child has died, like a little child, scared and hopeless in need of care and a need to feel safe. We are not broken, and we don't need fixing. In your own struggle to assist us, you may think it is up to you to 'make it all better' in some way. Let me put you at ease. It isn't. You may only be feeling that or thinking that, because that might have been your role as a young person, in your family of origin. So, if you ever feel uncomfortable approaching your friend, or work colleague because you don't know what to say or feel uncomfortable, don't be scared. Just think of us as a little child, we just need you to 'be there'.

I hope this section really helps you, our friends, because you see us at our worst and that can be challenging for you.

Just your acknowledgement of what has happened. Just a hug, a big one means so much to us rather than looking away, or crossing the street, because it is too painful for YOU because you don't know what to say or do. It takes courage from you to face what we are facing; imagine how we feel. It means so much. The renowned scholar and author Paul Fussell once said: *'The real reason that soldiers fall silent is that soldiers have discovered no-one is really interested in the bad news they have to report. What listener wants to be torn and shaken when he doesn't have to be?'*

So, what can I do you ask? It is so simple:

- A hug. Just hug me as if you will never let me go, and do not release me until I release you first
- Just listen (the quote that follows explains this beautifully) just nod and hug us
- Just sit with me. Watch a movie. Hold my hand
- We may or may not want to 'talk'. If we do, we may want to just say something simple as, 'I miss her or him.' This can be difficult for you as a friend, because you may take that as a signal that we may want to have a big chat about it as it could have been the first time we have opened up. To

check this out, all you need to say is, 'It must be so painful for you, do you want to tell me more?' If they say no. It's ok we are just taking small steps.

> *'Deep listening can help and relieve the suffering from the other person. It is called compassionate listening. You listen with only one purpose; help him or her to empty his heart, even if he says wrong things, bad things (curses or swears) 'wild talk' or says things full of wrong perceptions. If you want to help him or her to correct their perception, you wait for another time just listening like that can bring transformation and healing.'*
> Thich Nhat Hanh

Compassionate listening is harder than you think. To just sit and listen without responding can make such a difference to our healing.

I want to jump in here early and say, loud and clear, there is no place and no time for any tough love when a friend or family member has lost their child, no matter what age they are. We just need to feel understood and loved for who we are, right now in this space in this time. Not criticised, not judged, not told to snap out of it, or that 'we should be over it'.

There are three reasons for this:

- If you have lost a child yourself, those words wouldn't even cross your lips.
- Those comments show a lack of understanding and if anything, will cause us to regress 'big time' – right now we are just trying to make it through the day, so please be kind and patient.

- We do not need an opinion on our status unless we ask for it. Please say nothing just be present to us, that can make so much of a difference to our healing process.

To be understood

Our brain is trying to understand the situation. It can take years to move forward to acceptance if we don't get the right support. We need our friends more than ever. I would like to share another family story with you. It's about my cousin who passed away 15 years ago, was diagnosed with terminal cancer.

He unexpectedly collapsed while he was at the supermarket and was taken to the hospital in an ambulance. After three weeks of tests and scans it was discovered he had eight brain tumours. He had to face the fact that he only had 12 months to live. He was only 40 years of age trying to digest this information, and of course, everyone that knew that he collapsed, wanted to know what was the cause. When he did tell his friends, they all fell apart. He was the one, who was consoling them, rather than the other way around.

I will always remember the day he rang me and told me this news. When I heard his voice, he sounded so alone and distant, I held back the tears and was so glad I did because he said, 'Cuz, it's Steve, I have some bad news. And before you say or do anything, please Wendy, please, don't cry, just don't. I can't deal with it. Everyone I have spoken to is crying around me and making me feel miserable. I need you to be "normal", please be normal with me.' I agreed, and he hit me with it. 'I've got 12 months to live at best.'

I remember just saying the most inappropriate thing, 'Well, we have got a lot of living to do then before you pop off!' He laughed, saying,

'I needed that.' It wasn't until I got off the phone that I sobbed my heart out. Forty is too young to die! He had children, young children, that still needed their dad. All I could think of, was, what if this was me? What would it be like for my family? The reality was, I had to put my own feelings aside. I needed to be there for him.

So, as hard as it is my friend, we need you to try and be 'normal' with us.

Ellen DeGeneres said that someone once said to her, *'It is one thing to be loved, it is another to be understood.'*

Painful comments – What 'NOT' to say!
- God needed another angel in heaven
- It was probably better that she didn't live. Her condition would have taken up your freedom and time
- You will be able to have more children
- You need to pray harder. Keep asking and God, he will hear your prayers
- You'll get over it in time, time is a great healer – Bleep off!
- Are you not over it yet? You shouldn't be overly sad; it is not healthy
- Don't say you understand unless a child of yours has died. You can say instead 'I appreciate this must be difficult for you.' (The words you choose really does make such a difference).

What can you do for a grieving friend?
- If they don't have this book – buy one or two – one for mum one for dad and put a ribbon around it. They will thank you for it! (Note this will also be available on Audible soon, if not already).
- They may not want to be alone, so if it is viable for you to stay over for a night or a few days, ask if they'd like this

- Send a card with a beautiful verse or affirmation
- Just phone and say, 'I am thinking of you' (it doesn't have to be a long conversation)
- Deliver a home cooked meal, snacks or baked goods
- Send a warm cuddly blanket (in the early days we just wanted to cuddle up and sleep)
- Create a roster with friends to help clean their home
- Take them for a walk on a nature track or at the beach – make it a fortnightly or monthly event
- Go for a drive together
- Take them to the cinema
- Visit them and bring over a movie and ice-cream
- Buy some scented candles
- If they have a bath, buy some bath salts
- Keep in contact, especially after the first few weeks
- Pop in for a cup of tea (but you make the tea) honestly it only has to be a quick visit 15 minutes. It tells us you are thinking of us and care
- Take some flowers out of your garden
- Take them to a show
- Give them lots of hugs
- Invite them over for dinner and pick them up and drop them off (sometimes the effort in the early days of going anywhere can be difficult)
- Give a gift voucher for a massage or hair appointment
- Deliver a basket of snacks.
- Just spend time with us

If you are an employer (and if your business can allow it) offer extended paid leave or the option to come back part-time in the early stages of our journey. This can be of great comfort, the tiredness and exhaustion that seems to overtake your body is something else. And finally, when we can return to work, it would be great to have a work colleague accompany us on our first day back, or at least have this offered to us. Just having that support person with you can really help. Relationships are the key to healing.

Studies show that having a good support network constitutes the single most powerful protection against becoming traumatised. A cherished friend can play a critical role in helping you heal.

Note: To really understand the effects of trauma and what constitutes PTSD (Post Traumatic Syndrome Disorder) – see Chapter 4 'The Spectrum of Trauma' from the book *What Happened to You,* written by Dr B Perry and co-authored by Oprah Winfrey.

> 'Become kind to one another, tenderly compassionate.'
> Ephesians 4: 32
> (The new world translation of the Holy Scriptures)

THE MISSING PIECE

LESSON 3

Understanding Trauma

*'Trauma is the ultimate experience of
"This will last forever".'*
Bessel van der Kolk

Am I suffering from a trauma?
An explanation at last! Thank goodness I am not going mad. I am having a reasonable reaction to 'what happened to me'!

Do you know how liberating it was to finally read information from an expert explaining that everything I had been feeling, thinking and going through for the last 30 years was normal! Before reading this, I was resigned to the fact that I was always going to feel and be this way, until my dying days.

I literally came across this information by accident, as part of my 'Emotional Intimacy' course through the International Coaching Institute in Australia. One of my lessons for further study and research, recommended that I read *The Body Keeps the Score* by

Bessel van der Kolk to learn what happens to our bodies when we supress our feelings and emotions. I had no idea that this book was going to be a game changer for me. It was about trauma survivors and what they had experienced. Voilà there it all was, written down, every symptom I was feeling. I can't tell you how elated I was to discover this new knowledge.

The suffering in silence can now come to an end. I don't have to develop strategies to survive and pretend that everything was honky dory. It was the first time in years that I really cried; I mean really cried. I believed I not only cried for my own self, but for my grandma too. No-one was able to reassure her that she wasn't going mad, and that what she was feeling was completely normal. The sense of relief is hard to put into words. How alone she must have felt. For me, it was if I had found the missing piece of the puzzle to my soul. A massive weight had been lifted from my shoulders.

These are some of the feelings I was experiencing. Can you relate to any of these?

- Afraid of feeling
- Helplessness
- Your heart races
- Heartbroken
- Distracted, trouble focusing and prioritising
- Anxiety
- Depression
- Self-loathing
- Nightmares/flashbacks
- Foggy brain
- Shutdown
- Numb
- Feeling you are physically and mentally vacant in a body

- Exhaustion
- Disengaged with your surroundings
- Tense in your shoulders, back and muscle pain, grinding your teeth and clenching your jaw
- On high alert for the next attack – hypervigilance

You know as well as I do how exhausting it is staying in survival mode. It is hard to feel safe in your body and surroundings.

Trauma is not just a bad experience or memory – it is as if we are reliving the memory every day. Trauma physically changes the brain. Even though you know the event is over, the brain doesn't know that it is over. The body stays in a state of constant high alert, you feel like there is impending danger, you are in fight, flight or freeze and when you are constantly in this state it is very hard to take in new information or new experiences. For anyone to judge or shame us and say that we should not be feeling like this because it happened a long time ago, does not understand that this has nothing to do with the rational part of the brain. This is not a problem you can rationally solve. This is because it has to do with the lower part of the brain, the housekeeping part of the brain, which cannot think rationally or understand the concept of time.

The interesting thing to learn is that trauma and the research of it, is relatively new. Twenty years ago, the effects of trauma were not completely understood, but with dedicated doctors such as Dr Bessel van der Kolk and Dr Bruce Perry, and the development of technology enabling brain scans, today, doctors are becoming more aware of the effects of trauma on the brain and body.

So who are Dr Perry and Dr van der Kolk?

Why Me?

Dr Bruce D Perry MD, PhD

Dr Bruce Perry trained as a neuroscientist and has been studying the brain and stress response systems since he was in college. He is also a psychiatrist, a field he pursued after his training in the neurosciences and is a renowned brain development and trauma expert. He found that having a brain-aware perspective helped him to better understand people. He found that *'seemingly senseless behaviour, makes sense, once you look at what is behind it'*.

In his book *What Happened To You?* (co-authored with Oprah Winfrey), Dr Perry discusses how trauma affects the brain. Since the brain is a part of us that allows us to think, feel and act, he wonders about what has happened to a person that influences how their brain works. Why did they do that? What would make them act this way? His book provides a window of understanding about the complexities of the brain, how the brain processes information and the effects of trauma. It is a must read or you can listen to it on Audible!

Dr Bessel van der Kolk MD

The author of *The New York Times* best seller, *The Body Keeps The Score*, Dr Bessel van der Kolk MD was born in 1943, and is a psychiatrist, author, researcher and educator based in the United States. He is a leading expert in the treatment of trauma, especially when it comes to how trauma affects the brain, body and nervous system.

For an insightful yet easy listen regarding the impacts of trauma on the body, go to YouTube to hear the interview between Dr van der Kolk and Matt Bodnar on **Healing trauma – How to feel safe in your own body** *The Science of Success – Interview with Dr Bessel van der Kolk* https://www.youtube.com/watch?v=kXv4WobnwyI

LESSON 4

How our Brain is Organised and Developed

> 'A good coach can change a game, but a great coach can change a life.'
> John Wooden

What builds the foundation of the organising brain?

Love, love, love ...

The way our brain is shaped is dependent on our earliest relationships. How our needs were met as an infant is pivotal during the first years of life in building the brain's structure. Much like constructing a house, if crucial elements are compromised such as the foundation, framing, wiring and plumbing in a house, it will only be a matter of time before any hidden problems will be revealed.

This means that early life experiences have a powerful impact on how the brain is moulded.

Why? It is because our brain is organised to ACT and FEEL first before we THINK.

Have you noticed that if you unexpectedly touch something hot, your body's reaction is to instantly pull away – or if your child goes to do something such as step out on the road you instantly grab the child? That is because your brain is designed to act and feel first. The same goes for the developing infant.

Your personal history and the people and places in your life influence your brain's development. The result is that every brain is unique.

In his book, What Happened to You? Dr Bruce Perry, a renowned brain development and trauma expert, explores this further. 'Our brain develops, sequentially from the bottom up; Input from all our senses – vision, hearing, touch, smell, taste – first comes into our brain in the lower areas. None of our sensory input goes directly through the cortex (the thinking part of the brain). Everything first connects to the lower part of the brain.'

To thrive, we need a consistent, attentive, nurturing and responsive caregiver. Why? Because what happens in the early stages of life will shape the way we 'think', and how we 'think' about ourselves. Consistent, predictable, loving interactions with an infant create a stable stress response system, while behaviour that is unpredictable, uncontrollable or extreme will result in an overactive and overly reactive stress response, which then shows up as behaviour issues and/or health issues in later life. Furthermore, the more threatened or stressed we are, the less access we have to the smartest part of the brain – the cortex, which can result in having outbursts or irrational behaviour.

How our Brain is Organised and Developed

What builds the foundation of the organising brain?	
Key – Principals The Pattern of Activation – Our stress response system Behaviour – Response by the caregiver	
A well-constructed 'house'	**A fragile house**
A regulated parent = a regulated child	*An unregulated parent = a dysregulated child*
Behaviour ❖ Baby cries – parent meets the needs of the crying infant. ❖ Attentive actions: Love, touch, attention ❖ Consistent patterns ❖ Predictable patterns ❖ Has a regulated stress response system – builds resilience to different circumstances. **Positive memories**	**Behaviour** ❖ Baby cries – parent ignores, gets angry, and shouts. ❖ Lack of touch, rocking or attention ❖ Uncontrollable ❖ Unpredictable patterns ❖ Creates an overactive stress response system – can be triggered by any of our senses for unknown reasons – is on high alert. **Traumatic memories**
Meeting the needs of a crying child helps the child get back into balance. This helps grow the neural networks that allow them to feel loved and then act lovingly towards others.	If you were treated aggressively or there was chaotic or neglectful caregiving, or you were not held as a child, your brain could be biologically affected.
The way that you are loved, shapes the important neural networks, especially the core regulating networks.	

Just as a poorly constructed foundation compromises the integrity of a house, disruptions in early brain development, caused by neglect or chaotic caregiving, can have lasting effects on our ability to navigate the challenges of life that lie ahead. The analogy suggests that a well-constructed 'house' or brain foundation is crucial for coping with life's challenges and storms.

THE CONSTRUCTION OF YOUR BRAIN CAN BE COMPARED TO THE STRUCTURE OF A HOUSE
'THE AFFECTS'

THE ANALOGY UNDERSCORES THE SIGNIFICANCE OF EARLY INTERVENTION AND SUPPORT TO ENSURE THE PROPER DEVELOPEMENT OF THE BRAIN'S FOUNDATION, ENABLING INDIVIDUALS TO CONSTRUCT A RESILIENT AND ADAPTABLE COGNITIVE 'HOUSE' CAPABLE OF WEATHERING LIFE'S INEVITABLE STORMS.

THE ANALOGY OF A POORLY CONSTRUCTED HOUSE EXTENDS TO EMPHASISE THE IMPORTANCE OF EARLY LIFE EXPERIENCES IN SHAPING OUR BRAIN. MUCH LIKE A HOUSE WITH A SHAKY FOUNDATION AND SUBPAR WIRING, INDIVIDUALS WHO LACK THE NECESSARY LIFE SKILLS TO COPE WITH ADVERSITY, MAY STRUGGLE WHEN FACED WITH TRAUMATIC EVENTS.

Summary

1. **Sequential brain development:**
   - The brain develops sequentially from the bottom up, with the most primitive parts in the brainstem (responsible for temperature, cardiac and respiration) then the diencephalon (relates to arousal, sleep, movement and appetite) before reaching the cortex (the thinking part of our brain).
   - We act and feel first, and these actions and feelings organise our subsequent thinking.

2. **Individual brain development:**
   - Personal history and life experiences influence brain development, making each brain unique.
   - The brain's key systems (brainstem, diencephalon, limbic system, cortex) organise and function based on individual experiences.

3. **Adaptability of the brain:**
   - The brain has a remarkable capacity to change and adapt to individual experiences in a use-dependent way.
   - Early life experiences, particularly touch and relational cues, significantly impact brain development.

4. **Analogy with house construction:**
   - Early construction defects, compared to childhood experiences can lead to issues later in life.

5. **Impact of early experiences:**
   - Core regulatory networks, developed in early life, influence overall brain development.

- Disruptive influences such as chaotic or neglectful caregiving, can impact the biology of the brain and affect functioning throughout life.

6. **Building a strong foundation:**
    - The analogy emphasises the importance of a well-built foundation, proper wiring and plumbing in both brain development and house construction.
    - Lack of skills to cope with adversity can lead to difficulties in handling life's challenges, especially traumatic events like the loss of a child. The difference between, collapsing into a crumbling heap or being shaken.

In summary, the analogy provides a comprehensive perspective on how early experiences shape the brain, emphasising the importance of a solid foundation for resilience in the face of life's challenges. However, as you will learn later in the next lesson, the brain can be rewired and retrained to overcome some of our learnt behaviours.

LESSON 5

How The Mind Works

> *'One of the biggest mistakes we make is assuming that other people think the way we do.'*
> Morgan Freeman

How do we experience an event? And why is it that we can be in the same room with a group of people, but we can have a completely different experience from everyone else? It is because, we don't experience the world, we experience *our construction* (our internal representation) of the world. We need to understand that who we are and who we are becoming is made up of moments of what we choose to do.

Whatever you do *consistently* is what will become wired to you neurologically.

Why Me?

Exploring being 'triggered'
Our behaviour – Our MAP of the world – Our filter system

So, let's map together what happens to our behaviour when we interpret an 'event'. Our internal representation system (IR) inside our mind is our map of reality and it is what we believe the 'reality to be'. We live only in our INTERNAL REPRESENTATION.

No matter how sure we are of our thoughts, it is not 'reality'.

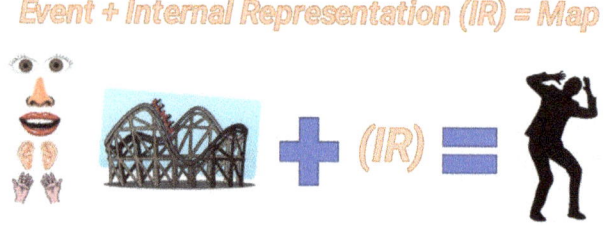

Figure 1. The event plus our IR equals our behaviour - © Copyright WendybKing – Life is Beautiful 2023

The map is not the reality, because your mind only filters what it 'thinks' you need.

Let me explain. We process events through our senses: sight (vision), sound (hearing), smell (olfaction), taste (gustation) and touch (tactile). Our brain takes in approximately two million bits of information per second through these five senses. Your nervous system cannot process all this information, so it leaves a whole lot of irrelevant information out and it does this through the mechanism of deletion, distortion and generalisation. (see Figure 2 on the following page). This is happening all the time, every second.

It filters through what we *regularly think about* or what we need. So what the mind does with two million bits of information coming through this external event every single second is, it will leave out all but 132 pieces of information, and then it will chunk it down to 7 plus or minus 2; a manageable chunk size for you. For example, how many times a day do your think about a food you love, or your favourite TV programme, or your body shape? Or if you have recently bought a new car, do you suddenly notice that particular make and model seems to be popping up everywhere? Yes! That is because what you think about the most, your brain keeps it forefront in your mind.

And yet if I were now to ask, right now are you aware of your clothes tight against your body, or notice the sound of the air conditioning, or the smell of coffee or the flowers on your desk, or some other noise or voice before I brought this to your attention? Your answer is probably no because your attention or focus was on something else. Stop and pause right now. Close your eyes and notice what you didn't hear, smell, or feel a few moments ago. What is happening now that you weren't aware of, or were 'tuned in' to?

So how does this work?

Everyone has a primary and a lead representation system that tells how they access their internal world. It can be through pictures, feelings, sound, self-talk or smell.

Add to that our emotional experience (or state) which is a feeling (sadness, joy, anger, jealousy, etc.) which is then affected by our senses (smell, touch, sound, sight and taste).

We then filter this through our:

- memories
- decisions

- experience
- values
- beliefs
- attitudes.

The most profound truth is that it is our childhood experiences that decides what our filters will be, which cause us to generalise, distort or delete information. Our filters determine what information we let in. We then respond to the event, through all of these influences. Therefore, your thoughts and filters determine your behaviour or response.

Figure 2 illustrates how this works.

Internal Representation (IR) is created by

Lead Representation	Filters are decided in Childhood	Our filters decide what we let in	State Psychology	Response Behaviour
V – Pictures		Memories	Joy	
A – Sound		Values	Sadness	
K – Feelings		Beliefs	Anger	
O – Smell		Attitudes	Jealousy	
AD – Self-talk	• Delete	Decisions	Anxiety	
	• Distort	Life	Fear	
	• Generalise	Experiences		
		Emotions		

Figure 2. Our filters give us an IR of what happened. - ©Copyright WendybKing – Life is Beautiful 2023

The question is – was the event really as it was interpreted as a child?

How do you feel, knowing this new information? Now that you can see how our filters shape our map of the world, it is important that we update our filters? Why? Well is there a possibility that the event that we experienced as a 'child' or young person may have been different and therefore requires a different response now that we are an adult? You may have been bullied at school and were told you were ugly or fat. And maybe the person bullying you was of another nationality and his name was Fred. What can the result of this experience be? One, you believe that what this person said is true, that you 'are fat and ugly', two that you believe everyone of that nationality is mean, and thirdly you loath anyone you meet called Fred. See why it is important to check our filters.

Check in with yourself:

1. Are you really fat? No. And if you did say yes, why would you let the words of someone that you haven't seen for 20 or 30 years occupy your head space?
2. Have you made an effort to meet other people of this nationality to determine if they are all the same or not?; and
3. How many other Fred's do you know?

You need to be honest with yourself. I know some people have had a bad experience with a policeman or a teacher and think ALL policemen or teachers are the same. How can you honestly come to that conclusion unless you have travelled to every state in every country and met every policeman or teacher? Stop painting all people with the same brush. It is important to revisit and reflect how our 'thoughts', or any 'biases' were set up in the first place.

Let's look at what our filters are again and see how they can unconsciously affect other areas of our life. They are our values, beliefs, language, emotions, attitudes and life experiences. Some examples of unhelpful filters include a belief that you are worthless, or believing that good things will not happen to you. The flow-on effect is, that because of the belief of *'not being worthy'*, or *'not deserving of good things'*, you end up choosing poor relationships because you believe you don't deserve to be treated with respect. Can you see how our view of ourselves because of our belief systems, life experience and the meaning we give them, can impact the quality of our life?

New research from The Trauma Foundation shows that trauma is an 'experience' not an event – it is what happens inside of us as a result of what happens to us. It is our 'response' to the event, rather than the event itself.

If you have said or heard someone say, that 'they do not want to go there', it is because of a memory (and sometimes memory is wrong). The **experience/meaning** of what happened can have a big impact on your life now. The memory of the past is through the 'filters' you had at the time. Remember what happened to me when I looked at Regan in the incubator for the first time? My stored memory of NICU; had catalogued these same senses to Emma, when she was in the NICU unit, i.e., the sounds of the unit, the smell of the unit, the sight of the incubator, and a baby. And since your brainstem cannot tell time, or know that two years have passed by, it activates the stress response system, and you feel as if you are reliving the experience all over again. Your brainstem can't say 'oh that memory was two years ago, don't worry'. You, may see them as separate events, but your brain categorises them as the same. It can take a moment for the cortex (the thinking part of the brain) to figure out what is really going on.

As Sharon Pearson (Remi), founder of The International Coaching Institute says: *'Whenever your brain experiences the sensations of fight or flight, it creates stronger memories than it does when recalling good times. Disturbing experiences are chemically supercharged, they stay with you longer than pleasant memories do.'* Our brain is wired/designed to keep us alive, not happy.

The good news is, that if we change the experience, we can change the memory.

We can rewire the brain. Dr Perry reminds us that 'One of the most remarkable properties of the brain is its capacity to change and adapt to our individual world. Neurons and neural networks actually make physical changes when stimulated, this is called Neuroplasticity. The way they become stimulated is through our particular experiences. The brain changes in a use dependant way. Repetition leads to change and improvement.' As the saying goes, if you want to learn to swim, you need to get in the pool. Reading about swimming is not going to help you to be an amazing swimmer, it takes action, and it takes practice, and you know it won't happen overnight.

You need to be 'aware', very aware, that whatever you focus on in life, whatever area of life you shine your torch on becomes neurologically strong; whatever you do *consistently* is what will become wired to you neurologically.

'You "are" what you focus on.'
Wendy B King

Our mind is a cafeteria of thoughts
Rediscovering your Pristine State - David R Hawkins

One is not really ruled by the mind at all,
What the mind reveals is an endless stream of options, all the skies as memories, fantasies, fears, concepts, and so forth.

To get free from domination, by the mind, is only necessary to realise, that its parade of subjects, is merely an arbitrary cafeteria of selections, traveling their way across the screen of the mind.

One is not forced to feel resentment by a mere memory, nor does one have to buy into its fearful thoughts of the future, these are only options.

The mind is like a television set running to its various channels for selection, and one does not have to follow any temptation of thought.

One can fall into the temptation of feeling sorry for oneself or angry or worried. The secret attraction of all these options is that they offer an inner payoff or a secret satisfaction which is the source of the attraction of the mind's thoughts.

If these 'payoffs' are refused, it will be discovered that, at all times behind the thought screen, there is a silent invisible thought-free space of JOY.

This is an option that is always available, but to be experienced, it has to be chosen above all other tempting options.
The source of joy is always present, is always available, and not dependent on circumstances.

There are only two obstacles:
One, is the ignorance that it is always available and present; and two, valuing something other than peace and joy above that peace and joy, because of the secret place of 'Pay off'.

It is a cafeteria of choice.

Credit to 'the International Coaching Institute in Australia'

LESSON 6

Understanding our Nervous System

> 'Inner peace begins the moment you choose not to allow another person or event to control your emotions.'
> Pema Chodron

An altered stress response system

Are you sick and tired of being sick and tired? Do you feel as if you are treading water, just to get through the day? Or, are you in a constant state of exhaustion? Or do you feel that you are continually on 'high alert' preparing for the next thing that could go wrong, feeling anxious, living in fear and walking on eggshells? Or possibly, shut down, you feel numb and empty and feel like you are in a glass box as I described earlier in my story? Then you may have an altered 'stress response system'.

If your home life is threatening or in chaos and your work environment is also emotionally or physically stressful then this is enough to change our stress response system, to either become overly reactive or shutdown. It becomes 'faulty' signalling danger even when we are safe. It is like an alarm system constantly signalling fire when there is no smoke or no flames.

Constantly living in this survival state can be debilitating, and too often the strategies we use to cope such as taking drugs, drinking excessively, or eating for comfort rather than for hunger, only brings temporary relief.

For us to handle and cope with stress, our body and mind needs to be able to rest and recover. To find a place where we feel safe, where we can take a breath and unwind. When we have moderate and predictable stimulation of our stress response systems it leads to a more flexible, stronger stress response that builds resilience and helps us deal with bigger challenges that we will face in life.

Stress is not something that we should be afraid of – it is the controllability, unpredictability and intensity of stress that can cause problems.

What is our stress response system?

Our stress response system lies within our autonomic nervous system. It takes care of a lot of our automatic functions such as heartbeat, digestion and body temperature, but it does more than this. It also manages your survival and stress response, to keep you alive when your life is in danger. Its purpose is about having a flexible and resilient nervous system that can accurately assess safety and danger and respond appropriately. Anything new will activate our stress response system, whether it is healthy or not. A new job, a new house, a new town, a new boyfriend or girlfriend ... until that 'new thing' is proven safe and positive, it will be categorised as a 'potential threat'. It is no wonder you feel so tired!

**Anything new will activate our stress response systems, whether it is healthy or not.
Until that 'new thing' is proven safe and positive, it will be categorised as a 'potential threat'**

Our nervous system is made up of more than 100 billion nerve cells and is constantly relaying messages from the brain to our body. For most people the 'unknown' is one of the major causes of feeling anxious or overwhelmed and is made worse if there is conflict in a relationship.

What is our autonomic nervous system or (ANS)?

The autonomic nervous system (ANS) has two components, the sympathetic nervous system and the parasympathetic nervous system. The sympathetic nervous system functions like a gas pedal in a car. It triggers the fight/flight response, providing the body with a burst of energy so that it can respond to perceived dangers. The parasympathetic nervous system acts as a brake. It promotes the 'rest and digest' response that calms the body down after the danger has passed.

It has three general responses or states, which we can call the arousal system:

1. **Safe** – you feel calm and connected to those around you
2. **Mobilised** (fight or flight) it senses danger, your heart rate and breathing increases, cortisol and adrenalin is released

so blood rushes to your muscles (this is our fight/flight response)
3. **Immobilised** (freeze) when you are in an intense situation you may just stare, or be frozen. The ANS detects that the danger is so great it shuts you down. In this state our heart rate, blood pressure and body temperature decreases and pain numbing endorphins are released. The more stressed we are, the less access we have to the smart part of our brain – the cortex 'the thinking part of our brain'.

And then we have another stress response that the brain can rely on – the 'dissociative' response. I liken this stress response as the 'man with two faces'. Why? Because he can be the one, that happily daydreams, and he can be the one that protects us. It's the one you need to help you shut down from the environment in order to survive.

For a young child who lives in an unstable environment or has experienced a trauma, the only form of protection in abusive moments is 'to flee to their inner world'. That is why our childhood experiences matter, because as children our number one survival priority is to attach to caregivers. Trauma compromises our ability to engage with others, and develop deep friendships, replacing the need for connection with the need of protection.

Unfortunately, this can keep our ANS from functioning in a healthy, regulated, and resilient way and keep us stuck in a state of survival.

When our ANS functions well it moves fluidly from one state to the other. One minute mobilised ready for action and the other resting and recovering (see the chart that follows).

Our Autonomic Nervous System (ANS)	
Sympathetic nervous system (SNS)	Parasympathetic nervous system (PSNS) – The Vagus Nerve is the main component
Fight and Flight	*Dissociation/Freeze- Rest and Digest*
(The gas pedal in our car)	*(The brake pedal in our car)*
❖ To optimise fight or flight response	❖ To help us rest, replenish, survive injury and tolerate pain
❖ Increases heart rate	❖ Decreases heart rate
❖ Sends blood to the muscles	❖ Keeps blood in the trunk to minimise blood loss in case of injury
❖ Releases adrenalin and cortisol	❖ It releases the body's own painkillers (enkephalins and endorphins)

When ANS gets stuck in survival states, our biology shifts its focus from the tasks that keep us happy, healthy and thriving to surviving the immediate perceived threat.

So what can we do when the ANS becomes dysregulated, and how do we recover from trauma?

We can retrain our ANS. This is done best with the help of others, who are safe, attuned and are present to our wellbeing, and are emotionally regulated. Because if the people that were supposed to protect you, and care for you, instead neglected or abandoned you, it is going to take time to build up that trust. It will take patience, because when someone is dysregulated (that is frustrated or angry) fear shuts down parts of the cortex, the smartest part of their brain. We all know that when we are with others who are calm and happy it makes us feel better, but when we are with others who are stressed, angry or depressed, it makes us feel worse.

I know from experience that when you learn to regulate your oversensitised stress response, it is like the beginning of a new life. To be free from constant exhaustion, anxiety, being on high alert and other health issues is life-changing. To be able to say and feel 'I am no longer in a state of anxiety', is incredible.

Remember, it is going to take time, just take one step at a time. The most helpful exercises or activities we can do, is both mind and body work such as spending time in nature, walking, noticing what is around you and switching off to just doing nothing. Have you noticed how a dog explores everything when it goes for a walk? It takes notice of everything, smells, noises, people, everything! What about gardening, looking at each plant in depth, looking at the lake or river, touching, smelling and feeling, experiencing the moment.

Yoga can also help with breathing, and relaxing our stressed muscles, as can dancing, singing and helping others.

Use the next page to write down what activities you would like to do to slow down your overactive stress response, and where they are located near you. A park, yoga centre, a walking track, etc. Is there a community group that you could be part of and make new friends?

Doing these exercises also helps regulate the biggest nerve we have in our body the 'vagus nerve', or 10th cranial nerve, a part of the autonomic central nervous system. This is the longest and most complex of the cranial nerves. It is part of the parasympathetic nervous system.

What is the vagus nerve?

Dr Bessel van der Kolk describes the vagus nerve as 'largely responsible for the mind-body connection', for its role as a mediator between thinking and feeling. The word 'vagus' means 'wanderer' as this nerve wanders through the body to many important organs and imparts signals to the brain regarding their level of function.

It is the nerve that registers heartbreak and gut-wrenching feeling, you know the sensations when you get anxious and your tummy goes crazy, your throat gets dry, your voice becomes tense, your heart speeds up, and respiration becomes rapid and shallow. Or you get that feeling that something is off, you know that feeling when you have made a decision then said, 'I should have trusted my gut?' You really mean your 'vagus nerve'.

The vagus nerve is basically listening to the way we breathe, and it sends the brain and the heart whatever message our breath indicates. Are we relaxing in a state of calm, or are we in trouble? Breathing slowly, for instance, reduces the oxygen demands of the heart muscle (the myocardium), and our heart rate drops. Amazing isn't it! So now you also know why the way we breathe is so important to us!

Intriguing, isn't it? If you would like to know more about this, I recommend listening to a podcast called Commune with Jeff Kransno,

Understanding our Nervous System

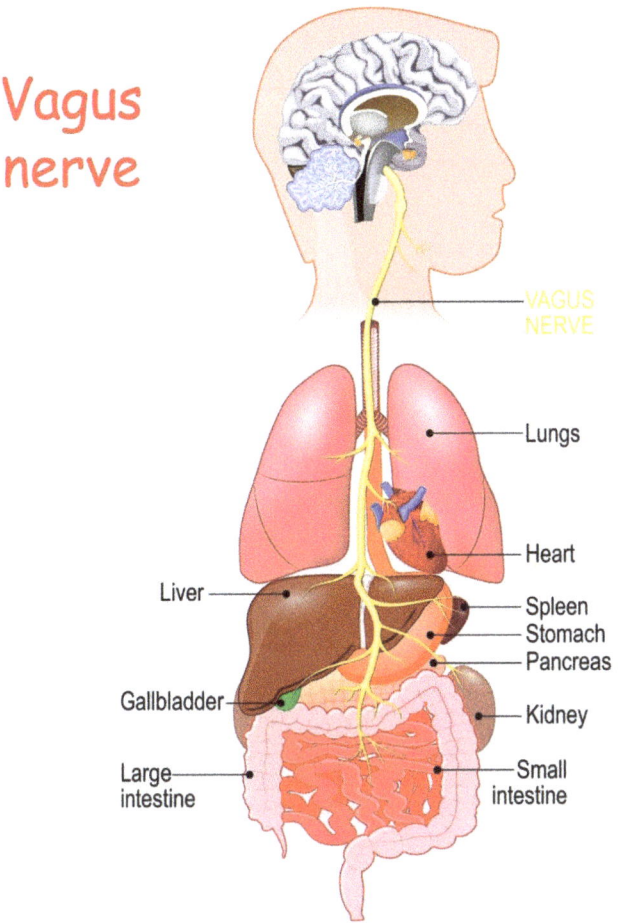

Vagus nerve

The Vagus Nerve is Largely Responsible for the Mind Body Connection.
For it's role as Mediator between thinking and feeling
The Word 'Vagus' Means Wanderer

IT IS PART OF THE PARASYMPATHETIC NERVOUS SYSTEM

Podcast no. 462 'The Gut Shame Brain – How stress and trauma impact our physiology with Dr Will Cole'.

The Trauma Foundation shares this encouraging advice:
'It's not about staying calm all the time or mobilised all the time, it is about having a flexible and resilient nervous system that can accurately assess safety and danger and respond appropriately. If we can do the work to heal past traumas and build healthy regulated nervous systems as individuals, families and communities we can end the cycle that continues to reinforce our greatest challenges and create a safer, vibrant and more connected world.'

We have an incredible body. Think about what the body does. Think about this: what, or who, created the body that we are in? The intelligence of the body is incredible.

I often think about this verse:

> **13.** For you produced my kidneys; you
> Kept me screened off in my mother's womb.
> **14** I praise you because in an awe-inspiring way
> I am wonderfully made.
> Your works are wonderful, I know this very well.
> **15** My bones were not hidden from you
> When I was made in secret,
> When I was woven in the depths of the earth.
> **16** Your eyes even saw me as an embryo;
> All its parts were written in your book
> Regarding the days when they were formed,
> Before any of them existed.
> Psalms 139:13-16, New World Translation of the Holy Scriptures (2013 Revision)

BREATHE

wbk
WENDY B KING

The Parable of The Butterfly

A man found a cocoon of a butterfly. One day a small opening appeared. He sat and watched the butterfly for several hours as it struggled to force its body through that little hole. Then it seemed to stop making any progress. It appeared as if it had gotten as far as it could, and it could go no further.

So, the man decided to help the butterfly. He took a pair of scissors and snipped off the remaining bit of the cocoon. The butterfly then emerged easily. But it had a swollen body and small, shrivelled wings.

The man continued to watch the butterfly because he expected that, at any moment, the wings would enlarge and expand to be able to support the body, which would contract in time.

Neither happened! In fact, the butterfly spent the rest of its life crawling around with a swollen body and shrivelled wings. It never was able to fly.

What the man, in his kindness and haste, did not understand was that the restricting cocoon and the struggle required for the butterfly to get through the tiny opening were God's way of forcing fluid from the body of the butterfly into its wings so that it would be ready for flight once it achieved its freedom from the cocoon.

Sometimes struggles are exactly what we need in our lives. If God allowed us to go through our lives without any obstacles, it would cripple us. We would not be as strong as what we could have been. We could never fly! – Author unknown

That story speaks for itself. Everything in life is designed to help you be AWESOME!

'History will judge us by the difference we make in the everyday lives of children.'

Nelson Mandela

LESSON 7

Family Systems

'Love is what we are born with; fear is what we learn'.
Marianne Williamson'

The moment I could hold Emma in my arms, my immediate thoughts were, I have been given a wonderful gift from God, and how could anyone think it was okay to hurt or abuse a young baby or child?

I could not fathom disciplining her the way I was disciplined 'out of love'. I was moved to tears. To see and feel the vulnerability of this precious child was overwhelming. I had another profound thought. Her life was in my hands. I am responsible for her care! She could literally die if I did not give her the attention, care and love she needed. The responsibility of that moment created a physical change within me. My role was to do anything to protect her.

My heart still skips a beat when I think of those first words, I uttered to her when she was in her incubator in the NICU unit and how she responded. Her little arms and legs went crazy, just hearing my voice.

From the second a child is born it is absorbing its new surroundings. Their environment and the way children are parented forms their core beliefs about themselves. There is nothing more important than the touch and nurturing interactions with your main caregivers, because families are the source of our first relationships. History tells us that children such as the Romanian children in care, and children in orphanages that are not held, rocked or shown touch, won't grow – in fact they can die and have died. These children, I am talking about, had a roof over their head, they had clothing and they had food, but they didn't have physical touch from their caregiver.

As Dr Bruce Perry explains, 'Children need their parents continuously throughout childhood. Parents teach their children the meaning of the world around them. The past 45 years have shown us how our families influence us, and our self-esteem. We learn from our parents, then we invent, and we pass on what we learn to the next generation. If we do not know our family history we may be doomed to repeat the same mistakes, such as beliefs, values and parenting systems that are not helpful for our emotional wellbeing or our relationships.'

Most of the parenting rules come from an era where every adult had to be obeyed, which was mirrored from kingly authority. We still have strong patriarchal and matriarch systems in our current life and legal and school systems. Family systems become chronically dysfunctional, not because of bad people but because of bad information loops. If you had parents that were born before the Second World War, you were probably affected by the rules set up at this time. The future of our world depends on what our child's conceptions are of themselves, and their views of themselves. Carl Jung once said, 'The most damaging thing to any family is the unlived lives of the parents.'

In my era, you never talked back or questioned a 'head' at school, because if you did, lookout, it would be a double punishment. Punishment from the teacher then punishment at home.

As a 10-year-old, I remember one of my male teachers throwing chalk and dusters at kids looking in their desk, whilst he was talking at full force, for not paying attention.

Some teachers acted as if they were God, with the attitude 'I am in charge and I can do whatever I please.' I remember in class one particular day, in our Social Studies segment. We were discussing the 'Aberfan disaster', a terrible disaster that happened in South Wales. My ears pricked up because I had family in Scotland. My Uncle Stuart helped pull out many of the children that died in this disaster, due to an unstable coal tip that slid down the hill and engulfed the school. Teachers and children were buried under the coal. I started whispering this account to my friend sitting next to me. You guessed it, I got caught talking (I was normally that girl in the class that didn't say boo to a goose.) Before I knew it, I was marched up to the front of the classroom, to get the strap. It was an evil looking strap. It had thin strips at the end. The teacher would step back and launch the strap onto your hand. I had seen this technique applied to other students before me. Their faces said it all. I was the first girl to get the strap in that class. I held out my hand and looked him straight in the eyes. As he was about to whack me, I remember saying to myself 'you bastard, may God forgive you and myself'. I couldn't use my hand for the rest of the day and my wrist stung from where the leather teethers meet. I felt like the teacher got some sort of sick pleasure from hurting you. I can just hear Matthew Perry from *Friends* saying, 'Could he have been any meaner?!'

It didn't stop there. There was a boy in my class who was left-handed, he was always being wacked over the knuckles with a ruler so that he would write with his right hand. How this sort of punishment or abuse was supposed to make you a better person or have any respect for a person in authority made no sense to me. But I think the biggest disgrace is the adults that were in a place of trust who were supposed to be God's representatives, such as some religious leaders, nuns and priests. In my opinion, this betrayal is unforgiveable. As we know now, many children have suffered terribly at the hands of people they thought could be trusted and have endured many wicked things that were carried out in the name of God, and to add salt to injury, when they did have the courage to speak up about this trauma, they were punished further for lying as it was 'unthinkable' that someone in such a position of 'trust', could act in such a way. For many survivors the psychological damage is such, they will never fully recover from these atrocities.

The parenting rules

In her book *For Your Own Good: The Roots of Violence in Childrearing*, child psychologist Alice Miller talks about the parenting rules that were used to condition a child at a very young age, so that they remained unaware of what was really being done to him or her.

These parenting rules are referred to as 'poisonous pedagogy', a term used to describe attitudes towards children. One of the patriarchal methods of keeping children in 'their place' was shaming punishment. This toxic shame not only damaged my own self-esteem, but many others. It harms the child's psychologically or physically. Alice Miller calls this process out as 'soul murder'.

Here are some of the rules of past childrearing that you may be able to relate to:

- parents were honoured and obeyed as if they were God
- children were never allowed to raise their voices or express anger towards their parents
- both father and mother had the right to hit and spank their children
- anger in children was especially forbidden and punished
- children should speak only when spoken to
- sex and genitals were shamed and heaven forbid if you even ask about sex
- children should be seen and not heard
- to question is an act of disobedience and so the rules are carried out
- one of the rules is that the rules cannot be challenged
- we are not supposed to 'notice' and have developed a 'no talk rule'
- children should *obey all adults* without question
- children are not allowed to say 'no'.

Does any of these rules, stir some uncomfortable feelings for you? Or maybe some bad memories? They did for me.

Research over the past 50 years has shown that these rules, although well intended, have had a huge physical and psychological effect on many of the adults of today.

John Bradshaw, therapist, author and theologian said in his book *John Bradshaw on the Family*:

'If you want to set up a child up for molestation teach them that. Teach them to obey any or all adults. I talked to molesters who have told me that. They look for the most obedient child in the playground. The child that is the neediest and the child that is the most obedient.'

Children need to learn to say 'no'. He further states:

'It is important to know that "no" should be celebrated just like when our child took their first step, or when they say their first word, because when they say "no" they are becoming a person. This is a little person looking up at this giant saying "no" or it's "mine".'

How many times have we read or heard on the news of the young innocent lives that have been damaged by people who were put in a position of trust or authority that have now been exposed for their vile acts? They got away with it because they had power over a child, knowing that child was told that they MUST obey anyone in authority, and they had no right to say No! These were children preyed upon both by family members, church leaders or others in authority.

The false self forms a defensive mask, distracting the true self from its pain and inner loneliness. The toll to the child is that after years of acting, performing and pretending, the child losses contact with their 'true self' and that true self is numbed out.

The most disturbing side of this exposure is that even though these children had an 'icky' feeling and knew inside that what these adults were doing wrong, they still felt at some degree that they were to blame for having this done to them. So to drown or cover their pain, they developed a 'false' sense of self in order to survive. The false self forms a defensive mask, distracting the true self from its pain and inner loneliness. The toll to the child is that after *years of acting, performing and pretending, the child losses contact with their 'true self' and that true self is numbed out.* Once a person loses contact with their own feelings, he or she loses contact with their body, and when a child does this to protect themselves, the downward spiral begins. They will often have difficulty learning and struggle at school, which leads to behaviour problems, and then in adulthood, they will be drawn to abusive relationships because it is safe – it is what is familiar to the brain. All of us tend to gravitate towards the familiar, even when the familiar is unhealthy or destructive. We are drawn to what we know, or what we were raised with.

We must learn from this.

> *'If we cannot become children when we are children, we become adult children.'*

We have to stop promoting family rules that destroy the self-esteem of our little people. A major cause of concern in our society today is that we have a large number of people who look like adults, talk and dress like adults but who are actually 'adult children' and these 'adult children' are everywhere in society. Inside these adults is a hurt child, and people who are hurting, transmit their hurt onto others. Why? Because their developmental needs were not meet as children. In a nutshell 'children were not allowed to be children', to be shown love or learn what emotional intimacy looks like.

Building emotional intimacy

> *'The level of emotional intimacy with ourselves, is only the level of emotional intimacy we can have with others.'*
> Wendy B King

Emotional intimacy, whether it is with friends, family or intimate partners, is about being present with them, and them with you, even when it is challenging, or you are in a disagreement. It is also about being able to handle disagreements without walking away from them, rejecting them, judging them, or trying to shame them. Focus on the behaviour, not the person.

Be the safe place your special someone can be without threat of withdrawal or condemnation.

What is intimacy?

- Being, available, responsive, open and fighting for their dreams.
- Saying 'I love you' is not enough. You have to SHOW ME. Love has to be expressed. That takes courage, being vulnerable and open to rejection.
- It is knowing how to handle conflict.
- It is knowing how to be gentle and compassionate.
- You do not need to be 'right' all the time.
- It requires saying 'sorry' and 'thank you' – it only takes one to start playing a new game.

The recipe of love requires a lot of ingredients.

Dr John Gottman says, 'In relationships, you need a habit of mind, that scans the world for "things to appreciate", rather than, "things to criticise".'

So now is the time for us to break free and question these rules and stop 'our pain' being transmitted to the next generation. But to do this, we first need to:

1. Learn and educate ourselves on how children learn and develop. Children can only do or learn at age specific stages. We need a better understanding of the developmental stages that form their solid self-esteem

2. Grown adults that have been scarred by child abuse need help and better education on how to work on themselves to resolve issues that still haunt them and are carried with them on a daily basis
3. Learn what love is and what 'emotional intimacy' looks like.

Anyone who does not have a solid sense of self-esteem will have trouble forming intimate bonds with a partner. We need to know how to take care of ourselves before we can take care of others. It is not selfish taking care of your needs. The truth is, many feel guilty about taking care of themselves. We need to re-educate ourselves. Once you know what happened to you, you can do something about it.

> 'The ultimate tragedy is not the oppression and cruelty by the bad people, but the silence over that by the good people.'
> Martin Luther King

The good news is that this can happen. Your brain is malleable, and you can heal from these bad memories. You can do this by working with someone who has been where you have and has done the work. If you don't get help, you will continue to be plagued by those inner voices that tell you that you are not good enough. It doesn't have to be that way.

As your mother, I promise you that I will always be in 1 of 3 places... in front of you to cheer you on, behind you to have your back, or next to you so that you aren't walking alone.

LESSON 8

Children: Emotions and Self-Awareness

> 'The way we talk to our children
> becomes their inner voice.'
> Peggy O'Mara

One of the biggest aha moments I had during my research, is how our brain develops, especially in the early-stages of infancy through to adulthood. You cannot expect a child to be responsible like an adult, it is impossible. A child's brain is not fully developed until approximately 28 years of age.

For example, I never knew:

- children up until about 8 or 10 personalise everything!
- they feel everything!
- they do not have the capacity to think logically!

They are biologically wired to act and feel first. Understanding this, makes it clear that we cannot stuff values down children's throats, they can only learn in ways that take their cognitive and emotional capacities into account.

The facts are:

1. The emotional brain develops before the thinking brain.
2. We are biologically wired to feel and act before we think.
3. Real full-fledged thinking comes last. Emotion comes first. Emotion is primary.

I want to share an example that I had a few years ago with my son who was six years old at the time. It was the school holidays and he asked me if we could go to the store and by another 'transformer' to go with his toy collection. I said, 'I'm sorry son, I don't have any money left to do that, we will have to save up for it.' His answer was simple. 'Yes you can Mum. You just need to go to the machine in the wall and put your card in and then the money will come out.' If only that were true.

He didn't understand that you needed to have money in your bank account first before it could come out of the machine. Another example of this is that around the age of eight, children start to figure out there must be more than one Santa, and is he real or is he dressed up? How can he be in the store down the road and how is he walking towards me up the street? There little brains are going 100 miles an hour.

We can appreciate that knowledge and technology about the human body is becoming more and more available than what was available to our parents' generation. And it is fascinating to learn about how the brain develops and what other important organs do, in order to keep us alive. But what is equally important is understanding that how we feel and think and the relationships we have growing up have an integral part in our overall wellbeing. If what was done in the past did not serve us well, or was outright damaging, we need to identify this. We need to stop going with the flow and challenge the attitude of 'that is always the way we have done it', so we don't carry any unnecessary pain onto the next generation. We should always be willing to learn and improve our own life and the lives of others.

Imagine this: it was only 100 years ago that doctors were going from a dead corpse to delivering a baby without washing their hands or changing their garments. What was the result? Perfectly healthy babies and mothers were dying of puerperal fever (commonly known as childbed fever) and it was a mystery to them. After some research, a Dr Semmelweis hypothesised that there were pieces of corpse that students were getting on their hands and that these particles would get inside the woman who would then develop the disease and die. Once hand washing with a chlorine solution was introduced, the death rates dramatically reduced. The sad news about this new discovery was that all of the previous deaths were preventable. If they only knew that all it took was to wash their hands and change their garments before they went to the next patient. We need to learn that every mistake every failure is an opportunity to 'be better' and learn.

The question is, are you willing to learn, or go with the status quo? Our children rely on us in every aspect of their life for survival, isn't it only right that we give them the best start in life that we know that will be advantageous to them? Sometimes as parents we forget to treat our children with respect. What do I mean by that?

I mean treat them with dignity, patience and kindness. Remember, they are experiencing something new every day and their brain is trying to catalogue all their new experiences. Their beliefs about their environment and themselves are reflected to them in our behaviour and in our eyes.

Be the adult you want your child to grow up to be!

For a child to have a sense of identity they need to:

- have good modelling and they need to be free to be a child
- to do what children do, play, explore, express their feelings and emotions
- be guided by the parent with patience and understanding
- to be able to ask questions, to check things out
- know that there is someone to count on
- have their parents' time and attention
- know that they will not be abandoned for being themselves
- be able to say 'No'!

To be able to say 'no' is a boundary. It is being able to speak your truth. It is not being mean. It is a protection. I was taught, 'If you can't say anything nice don't say anything at all'. Or never, say no to an adult! This sets a child up to have no boundaries and can allow adult predators to take advantage of our innocent child.

We have to help our children understand this. As Dr Seuss says: *'Be who you are and say what you feel, because those who mind don't matter, and those that matter don't mind'*

> 'Be who you are
> And say what you feel
> Because those
> who mind don't
> Matter
> And those who
> Matter
> Don't mind.'
>
> Dr Seuss

When these needs are neglected, children lose a sense of their own personal value. Again, our children learn with their feelings and their emotions. One of the emotions that was forbidden to many of us was anger, because it was considered to be sinful or bad. Anger is an emotion that is often confused with 'behaviour', like hitting, screaming or swearing – they're behaviours not emotions.

Anger is an energy and a child does not know how to say 'I'm angry'. They feel these emotions as an energy, they may experience feeling hot or feel like there heart is racing faster than normal. They feel different but they don't have the words to explain what it is. So, they need you as the adult to help them regulate this feeling. The danger is, if a child gets angry and then you get angry, you are then telling your child that their feelings are unacceptable, and they feel shame and blame themselves.

So here is what you do and how to do it. (You may want to print this out.)

Little Lucy is feeling angry and starts stamping her feet.
Acknowledge this.
How do we do this?
Stop whatever it is you are doing.
Give her your full attention.
Pause and get down on her level.
See, hear, understand and validate her.
Talk kindly and slowly. Allow her to respond to each of these statements:
- 'I can see that you are really upset'
- 'I can hear the pain in your voice'
- 'I understand that this must be ...'
- 'It's okay to feel this way'
- 'What are you afraid of?'
- 'Where do you feel it?'

This shows love, compassion and validation. If children have to suppress their emotions, they are denying an aspect of themselves. Don't ask to hug them until they are ready.

Children have every right NOT to handle their emotions – they just can't. They can't regulate them, they are children. They need you – the parent, the adult – to help regulate them. We need to let the child 'feel' the anger and then talk about what made them angry. Not the other way around. Anger is energy. If we don't do this, then anger presents itself as an 'act of anger' in waves of screaming and violence, because the emotion has been suppressed.

Our emotional needs are like our biological needs:

- to be understood
- to be listened to
- to be who we are
- to know that we matter
- to feel loved.

In the following story, I share an example of what this looks like (names have been changed to protect identities).

It was a Sunday afternoon and John was at his father-in-law's with his wife and 10-year-old twins Roddy and Brett for a Sunday lunch. John's father-in-law thought it was funny to make fun of his grandson Roddy's new haircut. He kept batting his grandson about the style of it. John could see that his son was feeling upset, so he took his son aside and said. 'Roddy, I can see you getting upset and angry. You need to tell your grandfather that he is making you angry, why and how, because if you don't, he will think that it is acceptable to keep talking to you like this. He will keep giving you a hard time, so when you go back to the table tell him what he is doing and why it is making you angry.'

John went on. 'But tell him after you have explained what is happening to you, that you love him. Do you love him Roddy?' He said that he did. 'Well it is important to tell him that after you have told him why and how you are feeling like this.'

So, Roddy told his grandfather how he was making him feel, and the grandfather burst into tears and hugged Roddy and has never baited him again.

By John acknowledging his son's feelings, his son felt validated, respected, and heard. His feelings mattered. What were the four steps?
1. To be understood and heard by his dad
2. Having his dad guide him on how to handle the situation
3. The grandad respecting his grandson's feelings and for speaking up
4. Being vulnerable and speaking 'his truth' brought him closer to his grandfather and at the same time did so much for his self-esteem.

It was never the grandad's intention to hurt his grandson, but when he realised it, he didn't mock his grandson for it, he apologised. That is what love is. Acknowledging the emotions and feelings of others whether they are a child or an adult.

Now just imagine for a second how else that could have played out in a negative way.
1. Dad tells Roddy to harden up
2. Roddy gets angry and yells at his dad for not understanding him
3. His dad yells back, 'Don't talk to me like that!'
4. The grandfather coming out to see what all the commotion is and seeing his son and grandson fighting when they should be having a lovely relaxing meal and time together.

5. Roddy screaming at his grandfather – 'you hurt my feelings!'
6. The grandfather being dismissive and saying, 'Is this what all the commotion is about?' and scoffing
7. Dad tells Roddy to apologise to Grandad for yelling at him
8. Roddy says no!
9. Dad gives Roddy a whack across the head for talking back
10. Roddy cries and runs off and says he never wants to come back here ever again.

See how different the situation could have been? You could cut the atmosphere with a knife. See the drama that was created! The question is? Who benefited from that response? No-one.
In comparison to the first way that ended in cuddles and joyful tears the second option ended in family disharmony. Which one would you prefer?

When we can manage our emotions, we teach our children to co-regulate and grow up to be adults that don't suffer from self-consciousness (which is shame-based). Emotions are not dangerous; our body is designed to feel everything and meet the emotion. Many are confused to hear this because this is what most of us experienced:

> 'If expressing emotion was shamed ...
> If you were mocked, judged or ridiculed, or ignored when you expressed a particular emotion, you internalised this to mean that you are "the problem". Whatever the emotion, it becomes attached to toxic shame. You may then exhibit the emotion less or distance yourself from it.'
> From Ultimate You by Remi (Sharon) Pearson

Emotional expression allows greater connection with self and others, and last but not least, it avoids unnecessary health issues or family disharmony that are being linked to suppressing our emotions and needs or living in a constant state of shame or fear.

One of the biggest mistakes as a human race, is being fearful of our emotions.

> We've been conditioned to be shamed for who we are.
>
> There are two types of shame. Toxic shame, when our emotions are shamed, e.g. 'You are a mistake' or healthy guilt shame, e.g. 'I made a mistake'. Notice the difference in the language.
>
> If you suppress sadness, you suppress everything – your 'aliveness' decreases.

Children don't say, 'I had a hard day, can we talk?' They say, 'Will You play with me?'

Lawrence Cohen

LESSON 9

Who Am I?
A Precious Child – We All Have a Wounded Child Within Us

> 'The way we were treated as small children is the way we treat ourselves for the rest of our lives, with cruelty or with tenderness. We often impose our most agonising suffering upon ourselves and later on our children.'
> Alice Miller

You are worthy, you are loveable, and you DO matter!
Whatever you think of yourself now, you had no control over how you were treated. No matter what happened, it wasn't your fault, no matter what it was. Not even if someone says that it was, or that you convinced yourself that it was. You did not 'make someone' hurt you. They hurt you. They are responsible for their own response and actions, not YOU!

You were shaped by your childhood. You did all you could as a little child to be safe, to feel loved and accepted. For most of us, our parents were tuned in to us physically and not emotionally because they didn't know how. They can't give you what they don't have. It is like you are fighting the air. IT is not an excuse; it is an explanation. As a child, if you were denied an emotion, you were denied being accepted for yourself, and you deserve to be accepted for who you are.

If expressing an emotion was shamed through being mocked, judged, rejected or ignored, you internalised this to mean that there was something wrong with you, that you were the problem. The fact is, emotions don't happen to you, they are part of you. There are no negative emotions. All emotions are within you and need to be expressed.

It is not uncommon that if you had an 'adult child' for a parent that they did not have their developmental dependency needs meet. There was no way they could give to you or be there for you, so your needs were met. We must be able to address our family without blame and see it the way it is. It is not our job to change our parents – that is a boundary violation. It is our job to be the best version we can be. As an adult you now have a choice to change this.

Everyone needs to know, that so many things happen in the developing child in the first six years of life, and if key neural networks do not get the right experiences at the right times, some essential capabilities will not develop normally. When we understand these stages, it becomes clear that there is nothing wrong with us. We just didn't learn certain coping life skills that would have enabled us to deal with relationships and a whole lot of other aspects in our life.

Our parents couldn't teach us, there was no way they could do it. You can't give what you don't have. The good news is that you can heal your inner child and be comfortable with all your emotions. It is very important to go back and understand what happened to us.

> *What is worse than not having a childhood?*
> *Also missing out on adulthood because you are still*
> *living as a child ... what has been the emotional and*
> *physical cost to your wellbeing so far?*
> *Let's start healing today.*

Have you stopped to consider what is important to you? What would be some of your values? If you are having trouble starting, think about what you don't want in your life, rather than what you do.

Have a go at creating your own family or Parenting Manifesto – If you want some inspiration, you can read Brené Brown's 'Parenting Manifesto' in Oprah Winfrey's book *A Path Made Clear*.

Our Family Manifesto

Above all else, I want you to know that ...

You will learn that you are worthy of love, belonging and joy every time you see me practise self-compassion and embrace my own imperfections.

We will practice (name them, i.e. patience, courage, etc.).

We will create a safe place for you to share your thoughts and feelings without criticism or judgment.

We will teach you ….

As a family we will have fun by...

As your parent we will play and invite you to...

You will always have permission to ...

Signed The ……………
Family

'If you have been brutally broken, but still have the courage to be gentle to other living beings, then you are a badass, with a heart of an angel.'

Keanu Reeves

LESSON 10

I Have Got your Back – Men Only

'Free yourself, to be yourself.'
BONO

I know what you are thinking: 'I don't want to talk about it!'

I know it's a guy thing. Right! It was the same for Bono when his mother Iris died when he was 14 years of age. How did his brother, Norman, and father deal with it? They didn't! He had very few memories of his mother. They were three men dealing with their grief by never talking about it. In fact, he said it was worse than that, they rarely thought of her again after she died. In his book *Surrender and 40 Songs*, he explains, 'We were three Irish males and we avoided the pain that we knew would come from thinking and speaking about her.' It was a difficult for him and his brother – and at 54 years of age when he was performing at a concert singing his song 'Iris (hold me close)', a beautiful tribute to his mum, he wondered why her loss still got to him. He even asked himself, shouldn't I be over it by now? Why does it hurt so much after all these years? Forty years.

The truth is, avoiding emotional pain doesn't lead to healing. It merely postpones the inevitable and often makes the pain even more unbearable. The model of emotional suppression demonstrated by Bono's family is a common one, passed down through the generations. It's the belief that men should 'toughen up' and not let their emotions show. But this approach does more harm than good.

Albert Einstein said: *'You cannot solve a problem with the same mind that created it.'*

I get it, it hurts, there is pain and there is suffering – suffering is avoidable.

I know so many of you were mocked for showing your feelings or were never shown how to manage or regulate your feelings. So you did what many of us did. You protect yourself by hiding away, or pretending that it didn't happen so you can carry on without minimal disruption. Because, in my past experience, it is like rubbing salt into the already painful wound. You may also be thinking, no-one wanted to know about my problems when I was growing up, so who or what has changed since then? Or maybe in your childhood you had an absent father, or perhaps you were told by a close male friend, 'now that your dad is gone, you're the man of the house now, it's your job to take care of the family'. How could you, you were only a child. A child... Your job was to look after everyone else's needs but your own, so why or how can you possibly attend to your needs now? It goes against everything you know or believe.

I see you, I feel and hear you. Your needs matter as well. Many people underestimate the impact the death of a child has on a father. There is this premise, that since you did not carry the baby within you, you do not have the same amount of closeness. This is not true. I also know that there may have been an expectation, that the needs of your grieving partner should come first, because she is a woman and is more emotional, meantime, who has been there for you? Have you just suppressed your feelings or emotions and just conceded that 'this is the way it is'? Or have you turned to work, drugs or alcohol to manage your pain to get some relief? I get it, it is a dark and tough place to be.

So right now, in this moment, I want to acknowledge your pain and loss. You have every right to feel, anger, sadness and fear. Your whole world and all your dreams have been tipped upside down. If you were never allowed to feel and work through these emotions, or worse still humour was used to replace the uncomfortableness of your loss, it can take an awful toll on you mentally, physically and emotionally. Feeling this way can play a large role in feeling depressed or even suicidal.

In the words of Dr Bessel van der Kolk, *'The challenge is not so much learning to accept the terrible things that have happened but learning how to gain control over our internal sensations and emotions.'*

Over the past 50 to 60 years, nearly everything we have been taught about our emotions, is incorrect, and goes against what science tells us.

We are biologically wired to feel and act first, before we think. I invite you again to go back and read the lessons regarding the brain if you haven't already. Emotions are not dangerous, our body is designed to feel everything, and meet the emotion. It is a normal bodily function to have and express our feelings and emotions. If you can't feel you won't heal.

Why Me?

You need to know that when men openly share their emotions, they become role models for young boys, showing them it is okay to express their feelings.

The importance is getting out of your head and getting into your body, because if you only try to change something on an intellectual level there will be no change. But if you don't have the intellectual level there will also be no change. You can't just do it from a feeling point of view as you can get lost in your emotions.

What you need to understand is that when you were showing your emotions in front of your father, it was raising his own insecurities about his emotions. How can he be there for you when he didn't even know how to handle his own emotions? He couldn't and because he didn't know how, he had to shut you down or mock you. You would have felt so alone. The thing is, it didn't just happen to you, it happened to so many other boys and young men. Know that if someone is feeling an emotion and it is painful, acknowledge it, don't dismiss it. Dismissing it is disrespectful. Learn how you can do this in Part 2, Lesson 2 - Friendship

Now's the time to stand out, be different and be you, and see what happens. Cheryl Strayed expressed what happened, when she had the courage to do this:

> *If you take that risk*
> *If you take that chance,*
> *If you tell that truth,*
> *The hardest deepest story within you,*
> *You are not going to step into the light and be alone.*
> *You are going to be surrounded by*
> *people who are there*
> *With you and say,*
> *ME too!*

Is it ok to cry?

You need to know crying is a normal biological function, period! What if I told you that Jesus a 'perfect man' the son of God, cried – would you call him a wuss? Let's just flip that for a minute. If he was a perfect man and knew that you shouldn't cry and that you 'should just harden up' don't you think he would have done that?

I am not sure if you are familiar with what Jesus could do on the earth, but he could heal the sick, cure the blind and raise the dead. The account I am referring to is in the Bible at John 11:1-44 where Jesus hears the news that Lazarus has died.

Lazarus and Jesus were like, best buddies. The situation was that he had been away ministering to people out of his town and his very close friend Lazarus was sick. His half-sisters sent a message to him saying 'the one you have affection for is sick' meaning Lazarus. They were the best of friends. You know that feeling you can have with one of your best mates? It came about that Lazarus health was starting to decline rapidly and his half-sisters wanted him to return home quickly, because they knew that Jesus would be able to stop him from dying because of seeing Jesus other miracles he had performed. However, Jesus didn't return immediately and unbeknown to him on his return back to the city four days later he heard that Lazarus his friend had died. In verse 35 it says 'he gave way to tears'. He felt sad, so he expressed his feelings. It was a normal reaction. Even though Jesus had the power to resurrect Lazarus (which he did), he was still pained and felt the emotional loss to hear his friend had died. His reaction was completely normal – he cried.

There was no shame.
If you really think about it, if we were only supposed to cry as children and not as adults, why don't our tears dry up at a certain age?

You have a choice to change your old behaviours if you want to. However, if you continue to remain silent and stoic, and you continue to supress how you are feeling, and you are fundamentally at war with yourself. It's exhausting.

Why? Because if you suppress it, you are not allowing your body to feel, which then creates suffering. You need to name it, own it, and feel it – like you want it to be there. It all comes from the head, you know that annoying back seat driver, tapping away in your head that is telling you 'it is not okay to feel this way'. You can start telling that voice to be quiet.
As we learn how we handle our pain, we can also learn how to handle life. While learning to develop a trusting relationship with your body, you will naturally grieve random things. This is where people say that I am crying a lot, and don't know why.

It is because you are no longer suppressed.

'Don't go through life; grow through life.'
Eric Butterworth

This will make the biggest difference, saying to your body 'it is okay to be there' instead of thinking, 'I hate this', or 'I am embarrassed about it'. If we cannot have a healthy relationship with our thoughts, we are not going to do well in our emotional world. Do you really want to continue this way?

We must understand and heal the wounds of the past, before we can fully move forward. The words of Iyanla Vanzant are so true when she says:

*'Until you heal the wounds of your past, you will continue to bleed.
The wounds will bleed through and stain your life, through
alcohol, through drugs, through sex to overworking.
You have to have the courage to pull out the wound and begin to
heal yourself.'*

In order to be healed we must come out of 'hiding' as it were. This means finding a person or a group of significant others, who you believe you can trust. My goal is to make this happen for many men, to have a brotherhood in a place where you feel safe.

The relationship we have between our ego (our thought process – our conditioning) and our body is everything.

It is a normal reaction to avoid pain or run from it. But think of these two examples. We may dread getting blood tests or vaccinations, because it can be uncomfortable or sore, but we 'know' that the pain or discomfort is temporary, and the benefits are a bigger pay off. It is the same with going to the dentist, we will usually avoid going to the dentist, until the pain gets so bad, we go. Then once we have gone and have the relief of pain, we say to ourselves, why didn't I go there sooner?

Let's learn how to get the emotion out of your body

Emotions have a cycle. Who cares what triggers it, just get it out! Otherwise the emotion gets suppressed. If you times that suppression 100 times over, you get humans who shut down emotionally.

It's like a washing machine cycle:
The wash cycle – you feel tearful, you cry, you may cry some more.
The rinse cycle – you feel a bit agitated and feel your emotions, and you cry some more.

The spin cycle – you can fall to your knees and it shakes you to your core, you cry and shake. It feels a bit scary, you start to move from shaking and crying to sobbing. You are releasing the tension in your body, you are helping it to heal.

Then the cycle has finished – you feel exhausted, but you have made it. Your body can get back to repairing.

- Feel what you are feeling
- Facing your emotion
- Being with your emotion
- Staying with your emotion until it is complete.

When we are able to do this, we are self-regulating. Confidence comes from the ability to self-regulate. Self-regulation is the ability to process life around you and 'respond' to it rather than reacting to your emotions. Reacting to your emotions is exhausting and feels like a never-ending cycle of stress.

Dr Perry says in this book *What Happened to You?*:
'If we truly want to understand ourselves, we need to understand our history, our true history, because the emotional residue of our past follows us. But that cannot happen until there is a tipping point of awareness. When we understand what the true human condition is, what trauma has done to us, that is when there will be a realisation that we need to do something different. This is awareness.'

So, guys, it is now time to break the rules ... it is time to break the cycle, to create a new path in your life, face the fear and do what you need to do. Are you with me?

When you make a decision to address and feel your emotions, amazing opportunities will appear in front of you. You will be accepting all of you. People will soon see you radiating from your soul, because for the first time in your life, you are taking care of you, taking care of business! Remember the adult elephant? You are now ready to escape from your old belief systems. Rumi said, 'Grief can be the garden of compassion. If you keep your heart open through everything, your pain can become your greatest ally in your life's search for love and wisdom.' It is up to you to choose if you want to or not.

> 'Do not go where the path may lead, go instead where there is no path, and leave a trail.'
> – Ralph Waldo Emerson

Resources for your journey: visit my website to access a free ebook called: 'Feel to Heal' to help you with your emotions.

LESSON 11

Anger, Forgiveness and Resentment

> *'There is nothing to work on,
> there is just stuff to let go!'*
> Wendy B King

The misconception about anger

Anger is an energy. It allows you to 'speak your truth', it protects your rights, and it stops you from being a doormat. It helps you maintain your own self-respect so that you do not betray yourself. Anger is a boundary. It means that we can have conflict and use anger in a resourceful way.

Anger is not a negative emotion, but what you can do with anger can be very negative. Many of us know or relate to anger as violence, screaming, shouting and abusive language or behaviour. You must separate that. Some people link anger to aggression. They are two separate emotions. Emotions do not have to be acted out.

You need to be allowed to feel and express anger. You cannot be human and not be angry from time to time. If we can experience anger in a healthy way, and have a relationship with all our emotions, we can get back to a baseline of joy. A great example of using resourceful anger was when Jesus was on the earth 2000 years ago. Yes, he was a perfect man, yet he expressed anger. Really, when and where I hear you asking? When he went to the temple to worship and found people using his father's place of worship as a marketplace for buying and selling goods. Matthew 21:12-13 says, 'Jesus entered the temple and threw out all those selling and buying in the temple, and he overturned the tables of the money changers and the benches of those selling doves and he said to them, "It is written, my house will be called a house of prayer, but you are making it a cave of robbers".'

Contrary to what we have been told, anger is not a sin. You can have a relationship with your anger rather than your anger taking over you.

If we keep it bottled up inside of us, one of two things will happen:

1. We end up having anxiety because we are using so much energy suppressing our anger, we are literally 'holding onto it'. Eventually, it will exhaust your nervous system, or
2. It can take over you, and then is expressed by yelling or screaming, rather than behaving in a civil or resourceful manner.

This can be embarrassing, it happened to me on a couple of occasions, and you end up having a conversation with yourself, *'I don't know what came over me?'*

If we have been holding on to different emotions for years that we weren't allowed to show, it is going to take a good couple of months for the body to heal, that is due to many suppressed emotions that need to be released. The exciting thing is that if you 'allow' these emotions, they don't get buried. That is the key – feel it and allow it to go.

Forgiveness – how can I forgive someone when I feel so hurt?

> 'Forgiveness is giving up the hope that the past could be any different.
> It is accepting the past, for what it was and using this moment and this time to help yourself move forward.'
> Oprah Winfrey

If you read this quote out loud three times, one time after the other, it will help you to let go. Letting go of what you wanted it to be and hoped it to be.

I used to think that forgiveness was accepting what the person had done and condoning the act, and that if we could not forgive, then God could not forgive us for our sins. This is what I interpreted it to be in the 'Lord's prayer' in Matthew 6:14,15 where it says, *'For if you forgive men their trespasses, your heavenly Father will also forgive you, whereas if you do not forgive men their trespasses, neither will your Father forgive your trespasses.'* I didn't understand that the true purpose of forgiveness is to stop **allowing that person to impact how I live my life now!**

Forgiveness is not 'that it was okay'. If whatever happened hurt you, it hurt you. The realisation is that many of us believe that we cannot be happy until you or they say 'sorry'. If you think this, you are psychologically giving your power to them, and you will still hurt. Surrender to the loss and disappointment and accept the truth. Give yourself time to see them through the eyes of Thïch Nhāt Hanh:

'When you plant lettuce, you don't blame the lettuce if it does not grow well. You look into the reasons why it is not doing well. It may need fertilizer, or more water, or less sun.
You never blame the lettuce.
Yet if we have problems with our friends or our family, we blame the other person. But if we know how to take care of others, they will grow well, just like lettuce.
Blaming has no positive effect at all, nor does trying to persuade by means of reason or argument.'

If you still feel stuck and feel sad and angry here is what I would like you to do, another lesson of healing.

I want you to find a quite place, where you can relax and think about the situation or the person that has caused you to feel this way. This is a good way to connect with your inner pain.

On the blank page, I want you to write a letter to that person who hurt you, again with your non-dominant hand – if you are right-handed do it with your left and if you are left-handed do it with your right hand.

Dear Johnny, or Lyn (whoever it was that is still occupying you head space)

This is what you did, and this is how is how it hurt me...

This is what I am feeling...

This is what I needed...

This is what is has cost me...

This is what I want to resolve it...

There is no right or wrong, just write whatever comes up for you, take 15 minutes or longer if you need to.

Once you have done this, you may want to read it to yourself out loud, or to a trusted friend or your counsellor or therapist.

You may be feeling some strong feelings as you write this letter, some people get angry, some people cry, whatever you are feeling is right for you. It may be the first time you have allowed yourself to feel and let go, which is great, but I want to help you do it in a regulated way...

Breathe through the feeling and be the observer. How do you do this?

The four steps of awareness:

1. Name our emotion.
2. Own it.
3. Love your emotion.
4. Let it go.

Awareness gives us choice. When we have awareness, 'only' then do we have a choice.

Have you considered this – what if the person who hurt you, or offended you is not even aware of your pain, especially if you never raised the issue with them? Sometimes people hurt you without knowing that they have and if they did, do you think it is worthy to consider if that was their intention to hurt you? If they have done something unknowingly, do you think it is right to hold on to a grudge or resentment?

> *'Having resentment in your soul is like drinking poison and hoping your enemy is going to die from it.'*
> Nelson Mandela

Make the decision to move to the pain. You can handle it! Pain is inevitable, misery and suffering is a choice.

Whether you like it or not, you have a choice, holding on to resentment is not going to change anyone's behaviour. So you can either accept if for what it is and let go of the hurt, or you can continue to suffer and feel hopeless. There are consequences for whatever decision you do or do not make. The questions are; what are you going to do about it? Are you going to turn the page of life and move forward or not? And how is this possibly serving you to be the best you, holding on to it?

If something has come up right now for you, give yourself permission to let go of the past right here in the now. If you need to write down what you are feeling or thinking let it out. Acknowledge how you feel. 'I am sad.' 'I am angry.' 'I feel very hurt right now.'

Elie Wiesel a holocaust survivor had these beautiful words to say: 'Think higher and feel deeper. Life is not a fist. Life is an open hand. Waiting for some other hand to enter it. In Friendship.'

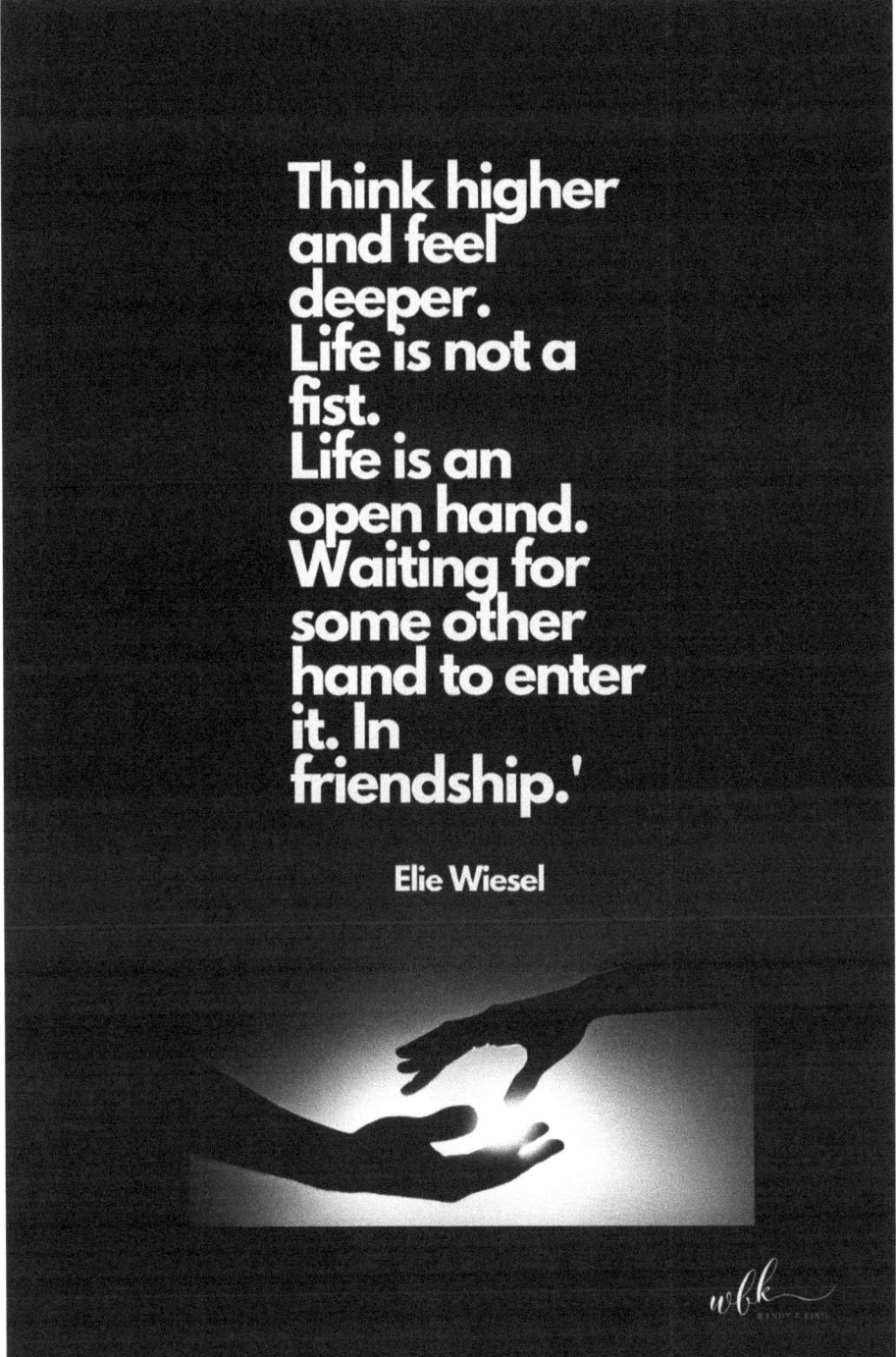

LESSON 12

Self-Worth is Your Job

*'Confidence isn't knowing that people like you.
Confidence is knowing you'll be fine if they don't.'*
— Brené Brown

You are lovable and you are worthy of love! You are! Even If you don't believe it or feel it yet, you can and you will. I can show you how. You do not have to sacrifice your soul to fit in.

I did not believe it or feel it for years.

My first realisation which I will never forget, was at the International Coaching Institute in Australia. One of the exercises (it was by Zoom, but it was still such a powerful moment) was when we were put in breakout rooms. If you are not familiar with this term, it means that you are virtually put in a room with a group of two or four people that the computer randomly selects from the attendees on the course. Within 5–10 seconds the other person or persons/s appear on your screen that you can talk to.

This was a two-person exercise, and I had the pleasure of meeting 'Michael'.

The exercise involved taking a turn for two minutes each, staring into the other person's eyes without talking, just looking into their eyes, then telling them what you saw e.g. sadness, playfulness, dullness, etc. You were literally staring into the person's soul. We had never spoken or met before in our lives.

I went first. I have to say, that staring at a stranger's eyes for two minutes and not speaking is quite an uncomfortable feeling, but this was a life-changing moment for me.

Then it was Michael's turn. He said that he saw in my eyes, playfulness, kindness, gratefulness, there was also some sadness, but mostly he saw a very loving caring person. It took me a few seconds to register what he was saying. My mind was going, is he making this up or is he just being nice, then I thought, why would he, I have never met him before. Then I started to 'feel' what he said. I mean 'feel'. I had been numb, shut down for so long. I started to feel hot. It was moving from my belly up my body, my torso to my throat which started to feel tight, then my eyes started to well up with tears and the tears began to fall, and my body began to shake. I was not expecting this reaction. Then suddenly the time was over from the exercise and we were regrouped all together again. Our head trainer, Matt, asked for feedback from anyone that wanted to share? What did we discover? What did we feel?

For me, I was trying to compose myself being in front of a whole lot of people on screen and I didn't want to feel embarrassed crying in front of strangers, but I couldn't. Unbeknown to me and all of us this was the whole purpose of the exercise. It was possible for some of us to be 'feeling' for the first time in years.

Michael had looked into my soul, a complete stranger and spoke his truth. He saw me for who I was. Those words set off a tidal wave within me. I sobbed for the remaining day, whilst trying to listen to the rest of the course topic. Thankfully there was no other exercises to do.

Before the end of the session, Matt asked the class again, if we would like to share with the class any new learnings from the afternoon session. What did we discover? What changed within us? What did we learn? What did we feel? I might add before the course started, Matt had said, for us to get the most out of the course, we needed to lean in and really participate, otherwise what was the point being there? He also said, 'You will be surprised what you learn about yourself when you are willing to fully participate and embrace the fear and do it anyway!'

So, I gathered the courage and pressed the virtual hand to acknowledge I wanted to share. I wasn't sure how I was going to speak as I still felt so shaky, and tears were still coming. Why was I able to do this? Because I felt safe and free from judgement. Again, a first-time experience.

I said the exercise that involved looking into each other's eyes, had a profound effect on me. It was like the first time I had been 'seen'. Seen as Wendy, not as a mum, not as a daughter, not as a wife as 'a person', a person who wasn't bad, who was kind, and I started really crying again. Matt said, 'I see you,' and allowed me (gave me the space), to just feel my emotions. He didn't rush me, he didn't tell me not to be feeling this way, he just validated my pain. He then thanked me for being vulnerable and sharing this with the group. Then when I looked at the comments screen, on the computer, I had nothing but, kindness and love from the group. They thanked me for sharing, because it also helped them feel that they were not alone.

This was the beginning of my journey to really healing. And guess what? I didn't die from embarrassment. I didn't have people mock me for being overly sensitive. I wasn't told I shouldn't be feeling that way. I was met with love, kindness and understanding. I am not going to say that I wasn't uncomfortable, because I would be lying. I felt very uncomfortable! This is how we grow. The lesson is that the uncomfortableness paid off.

Why did I share this with you?
Because, if we want change, it requires courage.

> 'Change only happens when we change.
> Things only happen when we make it happen.'
> Matt Lavars

We don't always get the love and understanding from our source figures, the people in our life that we expect to get it from. Remember, you can't give what you don't have or don't know. Just because we weren't nurtured or loved the way we needed to be, or felt loved or worthy, doesn't mean you are not worthy of love.

It takes practice. It doesn't happen overnight. This is the wonderful thing about our brain, it's capacity to change and adapt to our individual world.

This is called neuroplasticity. Dr Perry explains how this works in his book What Happened to You?: *'The brain changes in a use dependant way...a key principle of neuroplasticity is specificity. In order to change any part of the brain, that specific part of the brain needs to be activated.'*

So the question is …
Are you living a life that lights up your soul from the inside out? Are you in a job that gives you purpose, or are you living your life to seek approval from your parents or to 'fit in' with your peers? If you stay bonded to your parents and your 'old belief system' about yourself and you don't separate from the 'family rules or systems' you never become your true self.

You go to your death NEVER KNOWING WHO YOU ARE.

Do you believe you deserve to live a life that is in alignment with the person you are? The only way that we can find out that we are wrong about ourselves is to risk exposing ourselves to someone else's examination (scrutiny). When we trust someone else and experience their love and acceptance, we can then begin to change our beliefs about ourselves. We learn that we are not bad; we learn that we are loveable and acceptable.

Growth requires a little bit of discomfort and sometimes pain.

If we do not grow because of someone else's love, it is generally because it is a 'conditional' form of love. True love is positive. It allows us to be 'whole' and accept all parts of ourselves. Start with what matters to you.

Are you exhausted, isolated, anxious, not sleeping well?

What are you running from?

What are you hiding from?

Are you living up to someone else's expectations?

Are you using busyness in life to distract you from what you really need to attend to?

When we are loved unconditionally (accepted just as we are) we can accept ourselves just as we are. Wholeness is the mark of 'mental health'.

If you can't be you, then who are you?

This is my wish for you...

Comfort on difficult days.
Smiles when sadness intrudes.
Rainbows to follow the clouds.
Laugher to kiss your lips.
Sunsets to warm your heart.
Hugs when spirits sag.
Beauty for your eyes to see.
Friendships to brighten your being.
Faith so that you can believe.
Confidence for when you doubt.
Courage to know yourself.
Patience to accept the truth.
Love to complete your life.

RALPH WALDO EMERSON

Conclusion

'Extraordinary people are ordinary people making extraordinary decisions.'
Remi (Sharon) Pearson

HIMAD – 'Have I Made A Difference'

Prior to becoming a coach and author, I held the position of a financial assistant, and at the exit door of the organisation that I worked for, there was a sign above the door that perplexed me. It just had in capital letters HIMAD. I used to ponder what these letters stood for, or what they meant as I had never seen a sign like this before.

So, one day, I decided to ask my boss who (was the Financial Controller at the time) if he knew. He did, he said that he had put it there. I asked him why? He replied, 'It doesn't matter what role we play in our workplace, but what matters is that we are working as a team to achieve the same goals.' He put that sign there, so that when he left the building each night, he would ask himself, 'Have I made a difference to everyone's lives with the decisions and actions I made today?' I was left speechless. True to his words he did make a difference, because he died at a young age in his early 50s and the people that spoke and attended his funeral said it all.

So, I want to follow in his footsteps. I want my legacy to be, that with my own lessons in life and results, I can enable others to deal with life's challenges. That I have made a difference. A difference to anyone that has lost a child, or who has a wounded inner child, that I could bring a little bit of peace and comfort.

Maya Angelou said – *under every cloud is a rainbow*. Which is true. Do we want to focus on the raincloud or the rainbow?

Seek and appreciate all the small moments

I have been asked – if I had the choice of never having Emma at all, or only having her for five months, what would I choose?

The answer is very simple, I would never wish the death of a child on my worst enemy, but hands down, I am so grateful and thankful for those precious five months that I had to spend with her.

She taught me so much in her short time. She taught me about determination, courage, strength and to never give up. She also taught me so much about myself – that I am strong, kind, loveable, empathetic and courageous, even on my darkest days. That I am worthy of love and have so much love to give.

My words of advice: Never take your loved ones for granted. Tomorrow is never guaranteed. Love them like it is the last day you will have with them. Treasure the good times and the bad times.

Practice mindfulness: Mindfulness is not looking in the past or looking into the future, it is being in the moment today. Being present right now!

You are living and breathing now. Appreciate each moment right now. Be present in 'the present' while you have it. Many of us fail in this area. We disengage ourselves with the present if we are under stress and focus on the future. I heard this analogy somewhere. When you are in the shower, 'be in the shower'. Feel the warmth of the water, feel your hands massaging the shampoo into your scalp. Let your mind be with you in the shower, not in the boardroom or what you need to do after work. Be present right now and appreciate the moment.

What took me a long time to learn and feel? That I am lovable and worthy of love, that taking care of myself, and my needs is not selfish; in fact not taking care of myself is self-abandonment or self-betrayal. It is one thing to have people in your life that betray you, it is another to betray yourself.

My biggest learning …

This was really tough for me. Life … stop being fixed about how it should be, but you MUST go with it. Life … is fluid more than ever, you can't change the event, but you can choose how to respond to it! This includes letting go of how life 'should be', and any resentment. Focusing on healing, growing, and taking care of myself, so I can embrace life, and create a positive energy around me instead of a negative one.

We are all a work in progress. Focus on your strengths and the person that you are becoming.

Why Me?

Remember my Mantra about Emma… 'I am living for you, not dying because of you'. You have a choice – Love Wendy B

*'The most important thing to remember is, what happens to you
is much less important than
how you respond to what happens.
That determines your life.
It is NOT the "things" that determines what happens in your life,
it is how do I respond to it?'*
Brother David Steindl-Rast

As I was waiting for my book's first 'Print Copy' to be proofed; some wonderful news arrived. My first Grandbaby was born.

Emerson John King was born on 1 January 2024.

My son and wife kept his name as a surprise for me.

Emerson is the male version of 'Emma' and was named in honour of her.

My heart is filled with joy and gratitude. We have come full circle. My first baby to my adorable wee grandson.

As I have said before, you never know what is around the corner; Trust Life, it can surprise you!

Conclusion

The Rowan Tree
A Scottish Folk Song by Lady Nairne written (1766-1845)

Oh rowan tree, oh rowan tree
Thou'lt aye be dear to me
Entwined thou art with many ties
O'hame and infancy

Thy leaves were aye the first of spring
Thy flowers the summers pride
There was nae such a bonnie tree
In all the countryside.

How fair were't thou in summertime
With all thy clusters white
How rich and gay thy autumn dress
With berries red and bright.

On thy fair stem was many names which now
More I see, but they're engraven
On my heart
Forget they ne'er can be.

We sat aneath thy Spreading shade
The bairnies round thee ran
They pulled they're bonnie
Berries red
And necklaces they strang.

My mother, oh! I see her still
She smiles our sports to see
With little Jeannie on her lap
And Jamie on her knee.

APPENDIX 1

Scriptures of Comfort

*'Wisdom is a protection,
just as money is a protection.'*
Wendy B King

Have you been put off by religion and its hypocrisy?
How do you think God feels? He has to deal with the blasphemy of his name!
How would you feel if someone muddied your name or brought dishonour to your name? Answer honestly. You would be pretty upset!
Remember at the end of the day God is the judge of everyone, not man.

In Miss Maudie's words from the famous book *To Kill a Mockingbird* by Lee Harper, *'sometimes the bible in the hand of one man, is worse than a whiskey bottle in the hand of her father'* – meaning that if her dad (who was a good man) drank until he was drunk, he wouldn't be as hard as some men are at their best.

Every organisation can be affected by one person's words or actions in a minute that can literally ruin their reputation forever. Its effects can be far-reaching, damaging the reputation of others unfairly. It's the ole saying *'they are all tarnished with the same brush!'* But that is human nature, isn't it? I believe that we have all done it at one time in our life. We are pretty good at judging others, but not so good at forgiving. We can easily jump to the conclusion that if one is like that, they all must be like that! That is a very narrow view! But that view also comes with a lot of hurt. I understand that.

Have a look at some of these verses, and you feel God's love and see that he cares about justice. I have always loved reading the Bible. Just like many writers and inspirational authors who have been before us, there are many scriptures that I have found to bring a little comfort in times of distress. I bet you have some favourite quotes, similar to those that I have woven through this book. Take the time to ponder the words and how they can benefit you in your day-to-day life.

A God of comfort

2nd. Corinthians 1:3-7

3 Praised be the God and Father of our Lord Jesus Christ, the Father of tender mercies and the God of all comfort. **4** who comforts us in all our trials so that we may be able to comfort others in any sort of trial with the comfort that we receive from God. **5** For just as the sufferings for the Christ abound in us, so the comfort we receive through the Christ also abounds. **6** Now if we face trials, it is for your comfort and salvation; and if we are being comforted, it is for your comfort, which acts to help you to endure the same sufferings that we also suffer. **7** And our hope for you is unwavering, knowing as we do that just as you share in the sufferings, so you will also share in the comfort. *New World Translation of the Holy Scriptures (2013 Revision)*

Psalms 34:18
Jehovah is close to the broken hearted.
He saves those who are crushed in spirit. *New World Translation of the Holy Scriptures (2013 Revision)*

Psalms 83:18
May people know that you whose name is Jehovah, you alone are the Most High over all the earth. *New World Translation of the Holy Scriptures (2013 Revision)*

Romans 15:4
For whatsoever things were written aforetime were written for our learning, that we through patience and comfort of the scriptures might have hope. *King James Bible*

What happens to us when we die?
The condition of the Dead

Genesis 3:19
In the sweat of thy face shalt thou eat bread, till thou return unto the ground; for out of it wast thou taken: for dust thou art, and unto dust shalt thou return. *King James Bible*

Ecclesiastes 9:5-6
5 For the living know that they shall die: but the dead know not anything, neither have they any more a reward; for the memory of them is forgotten. **6** Also their love, and their hatred, and their envy, is now perished; neither have they any more a portion forever in anything that is done under the sun. *King James Bible*

Why we struggle to accept death – it was never his intended purpose

Ecclesiastes 3:11
God has put eternity into our hearts (that is why we do not welcome death)
He hath made everything beautiful in its time: also he hath set eternity in their heart, yet so that man cannot find out the work that God hath done from the beginning even to the end. *American Standard Bible*

Why do we die?

Romans 5:12
Wherefore, as by one man sin entered into the world, and death by sin; and so death passed upon all men, for that all have sinned: *King James Bible*

God keeps his word

Joshua 23:14
'Now look! I am about to die, and you well know with all your heart and with all your soul that not one word out of all the good promises that Jehovah your God has spoken to you has failed. They have all come true for you. Not one word of them has failed.' *New World Translation of the Holy Scriptures (2013 Revision)*

Isaiah 55:11
So shall my word be that goeth forth out of my mouth: it shall not return unto me void, but it shall accomplish that which I please, and it shall prosper in the thing whereto I sent it. *King James Bible*

God formed the earth to remain forever

Isaiah 45:18
For this is what Jehovah says, The Creator of the heavens, the true God, The One who formed the earth, its Maker who firmly

established it, who did not create it simply for nothing, but formed it to be inhabited: 'I am Jehovah, and there is no-one else.' *New World Translation of the Holy Scriptures (2013 Revision)*

God will do away with the Evil one

<u>Psalms 37:9-13</u>
9 For evil men will be done away with,
But those hoping in Jehovah will possess the earth.
10 Just a little while longer, and the wicked will be no more;
You will look at where they were,
And they will not be there.
11 But the meek will possess the earth,
And they will find exquisite delight in the abundance of peace.
12 The wicked man plots against the righteous;
He grinds his teeth at him.
13 But Jehovah will laugh at him,
For He knows that his day will come. *New World Translation of the Holy Scriptures (2013 Revision)*

Do not be quick to take offense

<u>Ecclesiastes 7:9</u>
Do not be quick to take offense, for the taking of offense lodges in the bosom of fools. *New World Translation of the Holy Scriptures (2013 Revision)*

God is the Judge of everyone for good deeds or bad deeds

<u>Isaiah 1:15</u>
And when ye spread forth your hands, I will hide mine eyes from you: yea, when ye make many prayers, I will not hear: your hands are full of blood. *King James Bible*

Ecclesiastes 12:13-14
13 Let us hear the conclusion of the whole matter: Fear God, and keep his commandments: for this is the whole duty of man. **14** For God shall bring every work into judgement, with every secret thing, whether it be good, or whether it be evil. *King James Bible*

Zephaniah 2:3
Seek ye Jehovah, all ye meek of the earth, that have kept his ordinances; seek righteousness, seek meekness: it may be ye will be hid in the day of Jehovah's anger. *American Standard Bible*

Why the earth is in a bad state

1st. John 5:19
We know that we originate with God, but the whole world is lying in the power of the wicked one. *New World Translation of the Holy Scriptures (2013 Revision)*

2nd. Timothy 3:1-5
But know this, that in the last days grievous times shall come. **2** For men shall be lovers of self, lovers of money, boastful, haughty, railers, disobedient to parents, unthankful, unholy, **3** without natural affection, implacable, slanderers, without self-control, fierce, no lovers of good, **4** traitors, headstrong, puffed up, lovers of pleasure rather than lovers of God; **5** holding a form of godliness, but having denied the power therefore. From these also turn away. *American Standard Bible*

Revelation 12:7-9
7 And there was war in heaven: Michael and his angels fought against the dragon; and the dragon fought and his angels, **8** And prevailed not; neither was their place found any more in heaven. **9** And the great dragon was cast out, that old serpent, called the Devil, and Satan, which deceiveth the whole world: he was cast

out into the earth, and his angels were cast out with him. *King James Bible*

God's promise to rectify death

John 3:16-17
16 For God loved the world so much that he gave his only begotten Son, so that everyone exercising faith in him might not be destroyed but have everlasting life. **17** For God did not send his Son into the world for him to judge the world, but for the world to be saved through him. *New World Translation of the Holy Scriptures (2013 Revision)*

John 5:28
Do not be amazed at this, for the hour is coming in which all those in the memorial tombs will hear his voice. *New World Translation of the Holy Scriptures (2013 Revision)*

1st. Corinthians 15:21-22
21 For since death came through a man, resurrection of the dead also comes through a man. **22** For just as in Adam all are dying, so also in the Christ all will be made alive. *New World Translation of the Holy Scriptures (2013 Revision)*

Revelation 21:3-5
3 And I heard a great voice out of heaven saying, 'Behold, the tabernacle of God is with men, and he will dwell with them, and they shall be his people, and God himself shall be with them, and be their God.' **4** And God shall wipe away all tears from their eyes; and there shall be no more death, neither sorrow, nor crying, neither shall there be any more pain: for the former things are passed away. **5** And he that sat upon the throne said, 'Behold, I make all things new.' And he said unto me, 'Write: for these words are true and faithful.' *King James Bible*

The Heart can get us into a lot of trouble (our emotions)

Jeremiah 17:9
The heart is deceitful above all things, and desperately wicked: who can know it? *King James Bible*

The heart is deceitful above all things, and it is exceedingly corrupt: who can know it? *American Standard Bible*

God encourages us to enjoy intimacy

Proverbs 5:18-19
18 Let thy fountain be blessed: and rejoice with the wife of thy youth. **19** Let her be as the loving hind and pleasant roe; let her breasts satisfy thee at all times; and be thou ravished always with her love. *King James Bible*

Values of God

Romans 13:9-10
9 For this, Thou shalt not commit adultery, Thou shalt not kill, Thou shalt not steal, Thou shalt not covet, and if there be any other commandment, it is summed up in this word, namely, Thou shalt love thy neighbor as thyself. **10** Love worketh no ill to his neighbor: love therefore is the fulfilment of the law. *American Standard Bible*

10 For whatsoever things were written aforetime were written for our learning, that through patience and through comfort of the scriptures we might have hope. *American Standard Bible*

Photos

Neil with Emma in the NICU unit on walk about

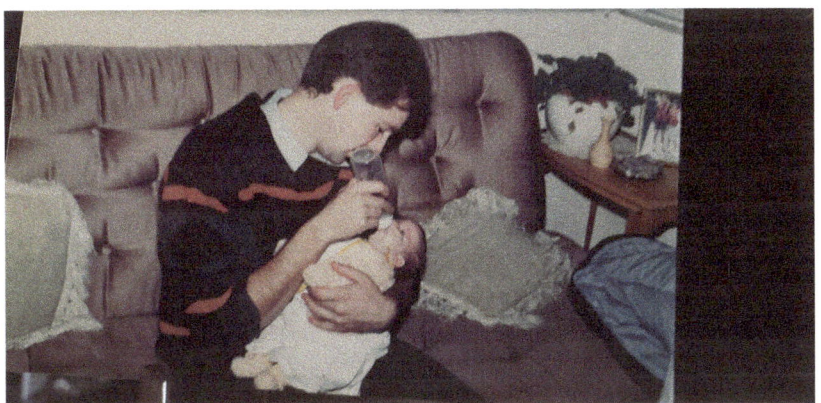

Neil feeding Emma a week after being home

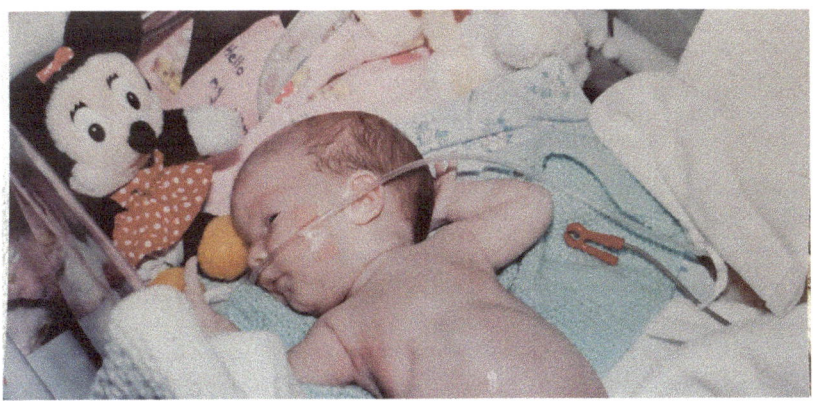

Emma 9 weeks old

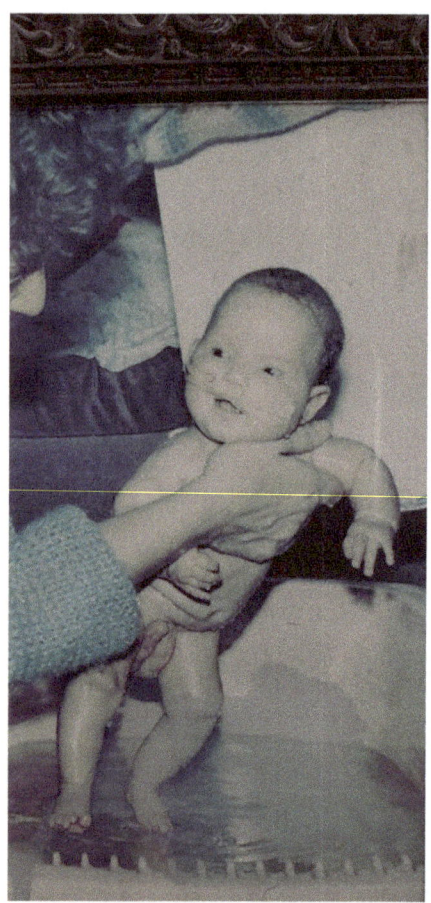

Emma - Just over 4 months old

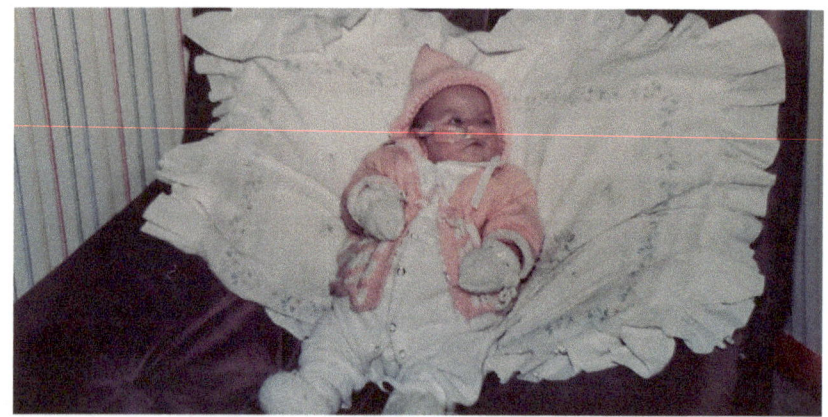

Emma - The morning before she died

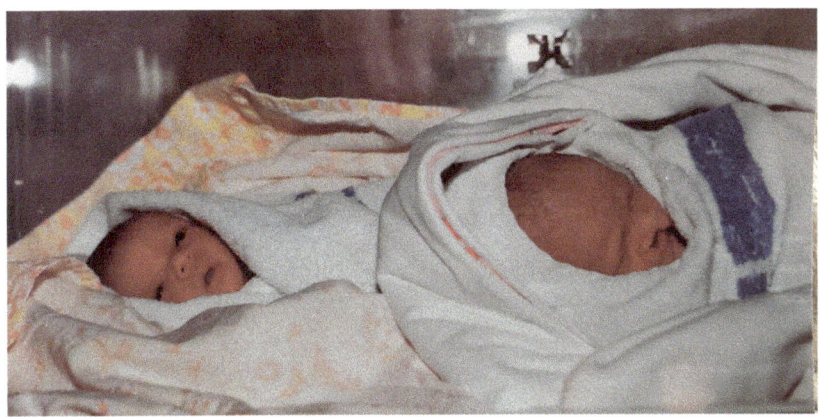

Twins one day old sharing incubator - Regan was upset

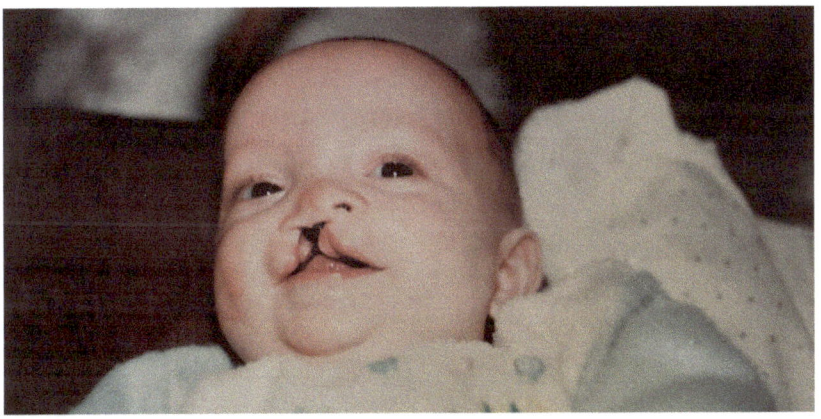

Regan - happy 4 months old

Author Wendy B King

Photo of the Children

Regan and Blair - Regan's Wedding

Mitchell and Charlotte – Regan's Wedding

Regan and Dr Jeff Robinson's final appointment after 21 surgeries

SEEKING HELP

Choosing a Coach or Therapist

'Emotional repression, is perhaps the most common symptom of our cultural crisis.'
John Bradshaw

Why do Oprah Winfrey and Hugh Jackman have a coach?

The one thing that people are never really good at is seeing themselves as others do.

A coach really helps.

A coach can help you see your 'blind spots' and give you direction in many areas of your life.

You have to find someone you can trust enough who can safely hold your feelings and help you listen to your painful messages. The relationship between therapist and client can be a healing phenomenon. Most traumatised individuals need an anchor and a great deal of coaching to do this work.

Ideally the therapist or coach has been on the receiving end of whatever therapy he or she practices. While it is inappropriate and unethical for therapist to tell you the details of their personal struggles, it is reasonable to ask what particular forms of therapy they have been trained in, where they learned their skills, and whether they personally benefited from the therapy themselves that they propose for you.

Choosing a therapist

Therapy provides the kind of modelling and mirroring that we did not receive from our caretakers. Ask them about their success in treating co-dependency and their belief in group therapy. Do you feel comfortable with this therapist? Are they curious to find out who you are? Not someone who just wants to tick the boxes.

there is no-one treatment of choice for trauma. The main role of the therapist is being interested in getting well. No therapist can possibly be familiar with every effective treatment, and he or she must be open to you exploring options, other than the one he or she offers. He or she must be open to learning from you. It is about making you feel safe and understood.

Feeling safe is a necessary condition for you to confront your fears and anxieties. Someone who is stern, judgemental or clinical is likely to leave you feeling scared, abandoned and humiliated, and will not help you resolve your traumatic stress. It is important that you can develop deep positive thoughts and feelings with your therapist to get better.

Therapy is a mutual exploration of yourself.

Getting support

Mental health services – Ministry of Health NZ
If you or someone you know, needs support, and you are worried about your mental health, or think it is getting worse, you can go to your family doctor or GP and they will be able to help you and refer you to your local community, mental health services or elsewhere if needed.

What do to in an emergency?
If you are seriously concerned about someone's immediate safety:

- NZ – call 111 or take them to the Accident and Emergency Department (A&E) at your nearest hospital.
- Phone your nearest hospital, or your district health board's psychiatric emergency. emergency service or mental health 'crisis assessment team'.
- Remain with them and help them to stay safe until support arrives.

Helplines

- Need to talk? 1737 – free call or text, for support from a trained counsellor.
- The Depression Helpline 0800 111 757 or free txt 4202, to talk to a trained counsellor about how you are feeling or to ask any questions.
- Healthline (0800 611 116)
- Youthline (0800 376 633)
- The Lowdown Text 5626 for support to help young people recognise and understand depression or anxiety.
- Alcohol Drug Helpline (0800 787 797)

Other Resources

There are a number of digital mental health and wellbeing tools available with ideas and techniques for looking after your mental wellbeing:

- **Small Steps** are digital tools to help you maintain wellness, find relief or get help for yourself, friends or whānau
- **HABITs Messenger** – (including Aroha Chatbot) a uniquely New Zealand chatbot app designed for young people – it feels like talking to a trusted friend. Download it from the app store on your mobile device.
- **Triple P Online** – online parenting support including Triple P. Teen Triple P and Fearless Triple P. Designed to help parents support their children and teenagers to cope with life's ups and down, promote wellbeing and make family life more enjoyable.

Suicide

If you have lost someone to suicide, there are lots of places you can go to for support:

Victim Support – offer practical and emotional support, personal advocacy information and run a WAVES program for people bereaved by suicide.

Grief Centre – offering counselling, support groups, brochures, books and articles.

Mental Health Foundation – offer a support website for people bereaved by suicide.

Ministry of Health – offer practical information and guidance for people bereaved by suicide.

You can also call:

- **Victim Support** – freephone: 0800 842 846
- **Skylight** – freephone: 0800 299 100

- **Lifeline** – freephone: 0800 543 354
- **Depression Helpline** – freephone: 0800 111 757

For Australian Residents – Getting Support
What do to in an emergency?

If you are seriously concerned about someone's immediate safety:

AUSTRALIA – call 000 or take them to the Emergency Department (ED) – they will not turn people away with a serious or life-threatening illness or injury.

- If you are not sure if you should go to a hospital or emergency department, please speak to your GP or pharmacist, or call Healthdirect on 1800 022 222 for free, fast expert advice. Hearthdirect is a 24-hour telephone health advice line staffed by registered nurses.

WHAT ARE YOU DOING WITH YOUR LIFE?

TIME IS TICKING

Are you Living on automatic?

In a world that often prioritizes external achievements over internal fulfillment, Wendy is a guiding light, reminding us that true happiness comes from embracing our authentic self.

Wendy's training and expertise were honed at The Coaching Institute, Australasia's No.1 Coaching School, where she emerged as a certified Meta Dynamics™ Coach incorporating the transformative power of Neurolinguistic Programming (NLP) into her coaching practice. Additionally, she holds certifications as a Certified Emotional Intimacy Coach and has earned a Business Certificate in Level 1 and 2.

In her coaching practice, Wendy addresses some of the most pressing questions that plague many of us:
- How can I connect with my partner on a deeper level?
- How do I say 'No' without feeling guilty?
- How do I let go of fear?
- How do I truly love myself, my body, and the person that I am?

If you are looking for your events or orgainisations next speaker, that will leave your audience inspired to take action, Wendy's most requested subject is 'Feel the Fear and do it anyway' Wendy is a speaker not to be missed!

WENDY B KING
LIFE AND MIND COACH

www.wendybkinglifecoaching.com   Phone +64 276 558 615

About the Author

> *'I am not what happened to me,
> I am what I choose to become.'*
> Carl Jung

Born in Glasgow, Scotland, Wendy immigrated with her family to New Zealand at eight months of age.

Today, she is a practising life coach and is CEO of her own coaching business **Life is Beautiful Limited**. She purposefully named her business this to remind herself of the gift of life and that we have so much to be grateful for, even in our darkest moments.
Wendy is a Meta Dynamics ™ Coach and has received and gained her training at The Coaching Institute, Australasia's No.1 Coaching School.

What is Meta Dynamics™?

It is the world's leading and proven based coaching methodology, and it is the perfect owner's manual for your brain.
Developed by Remi Pearson, utilising over a decade of experience as a highly successful and influential coach, leader, trainer, mentor and business owner and previously only available to private clients, Meta Dynamics ™ revolutionises the next level of personal and professional growth.

Wendy is also an educator, coach, spiritual teacher and motivational speaker who strongly believes learning, growing, having awareness, and knowing what our intention is in everything we do are essential to creating our own happiness.

Wendy's goal is to make an impact on how people view and see their life as well as help those who have suffered trauma, showing them there is a way through. She has invested thousands of dollars and has done the work and knows the way.

Qualifications:
- Certified Practitioner of Coaching. Trained to the highest level. International Coaching Institute, Melbourne, Australia
- Level 1 Meta Dynamics Coach – includes NLP (Neurolinguistic Programming)
- Certified Emotional Intimacy Coach
- Business Certificate in Level 1 and 2
- Member of 'International Coaching Guild' (ICG)

Wendy would welcome the opportunity to meet with your organisation, or any social agencies, nurses, or doctors who are looking to improve their own lives or the lives of others and stand out from the rest. A taste of areas of expertise:
- Why do we have difficulty communicating our needs?
- How do we create stronger relationships?
- How to live with trauma or grief? – Digging deeper.
- What is abuse?
- It's a guy thing, is it?

Visit Wendy's website for more informtion or contact her directly by email or phone for a confidential discussion.

About the Author

For speaking requests your budgets should consider, time, cost of travel and accommodation. The more information you can provide regarding your needs the quicker her response.

If you want to work with Wendy, either as a client or guest speaker, please contact her via email: wendyking@xtra.co.nz

Please note, due to Wendy's other commitments within her business, there are only limited 1 to 1 coaching sessions at a premium cost. Price is on application only and a 'Getting to know you' application form will need to be completed in the first instance. You can download this form on her website: wendybkinglifecoaching.com.

Acknowledgements

Thank you for my publishers Natasa and Stu Denman and their team for encouraging me, guiding me, supporting me and helping my dream come true.

To my editor, thank you for ensuring my book, my message, was written in a way to change the lives of many. Thank you.

To Nick Boskovski for creating my book cover, I love it!

To the many wonderful doctors that I have encountered in my life that have done and given so much for others.

To my friends, who have supported me along this journey.

To my family, who have seen the struggles I have had in the past, but who have also seen the brightness in my eyes and soul. To be able to heal and share my story with others, so that their soul can shine again as well.

- Dr Peter Borrie
- Dr Jeff Robinson
- Eithne McFadyen
- Associate Professor Kumara De Silva,

- Dr Carine Baker
- Dr Barry Taylor
- Dr Roland Broadbent - All the Nurses in the NICU current and past
- Ginny
- Mary Gamble
- Dr Astrid Windfuhr
- Bev, Graeme, Mark, Donna, Janell, and Rachel McLay
- Peter and Elizabeth Moroney
- Paul Rodgers
- Carolyn
- John and Julie Manley
- 'Hope and Sons' - Funeral directors
- Cherie Taane
- All our friends
- Our children: Emma, Blair, Regan, Mitchell and Charlotte

Illustration – 'Children want to play' – special thanks to artist and friend Heather Jameson – email her on info@followthewhiterabbit.com

If you loved my book, and believe it would give hope to others, please spread the word, share what you learnt, or leave feedback on my website. Furthermore, if you would like to see this printed in another language, please let me know.

Recommend Reading

- *Ultimate You* by Sharon Pearson. This book has helped thousands step into their true selves, and fall in love with themselves again.
- *The Body Keeps the Score* by Dr Bessel van der Kolk. Mind, brain and body what happens to our entire body, when we experience, trauma from war, abuse, accident or other life-changing experiences, and how we can heal.
- *Hold Me Tight* by Dr Sue Johnson. Learning and avoiding patterns that hurt or destroy our relationships.
- *Feel the Fear and Do It Anyway* by Susan Jeffers PhD. What are we really afraid of? Fear is a thing – so what is at the root of it?
- *Post Romantic Stress Disorder* by John Bradshaw. What happens to us when the love dies in our relationship.
- *Healing the Shame that Binds You* by John Bradshaw. Understanding what shame does to our belief system our self-esteem and self-confidence.
- *Homecoming* by John Bradshaw. Healing our inner child. For those who have grown up in an abusive environment or had to play a specific role in your childhood and the affects it has on your own relationships.
- *The Five Love Languages* by Gary Chapman. How we communicate our love differently.

- *The Path Made Clear* by Oprah Winfrey. Insights from many of Oprah's guests and friends about life.
- *What Happened to You?* by Dr Bruce Perry and Oprah Winfrey. An amazing book about the love you did or didn't get and how this affects the development of our brain and world view of life.
- *Follow your Heart* by Andrew Matthews. Finding out what true happiness is and is not. A new insightful perspective of what really brings you happiness.
- *At Home with the World* by Thïch Nhāt Hanh. Stories and experiences of those that have survived and suffered the effects of the Vietnam War.
- *Surrender: 40 Songs and One Story* by Bono. (I love the Audio!) – The loss of his mum at the age of 14 years old, his life growing up, his successful career, and his selfless acts as a humanitarian.

Bonuses

> *'The moment you take responsibility
> for everything in your life,
> is the moment you can change anything in your life.'*
> — Hal Elrod

Without connection we experience loneliness. We are designed to feel, love, touch and find comfort amongst other human beings. Sadly, this is not always the case.

If you really want some guidance on how to stop and reassess what you want in your life, visit my website for a free download called 'My Ideal Day'.

To access a free downloadable ebook about our 'Core emotions' or 'Feel to Heal' please visit my website: [www.wendybkinglifecoaching.com]

Coming soon:

My next book …

Online course : Freedom to be you (Developing)

Who are you? The mask we wear.
How do I love myself?
Setting boundaries. How to say no without feeling guilty.
Feeling to heal.
Emotions how to control them and they don't control you.
Overcoming shame.
What we needed, to grow into a whole human being.
Loyalty versus love – separating from the family tribe.

Notes

Why Me?

Notes

www.ingramcontent.com/pod-product-compliance
Lightning Source LLC
Chambersburg PA
CBHW041304110526
44590CB00028B/4241